Humanistic Studies in The Communication Arts

GEORGE N. GORDON, General Editor

A TAXONOMY OF
CONCEPTS IN COMMUNICATION

D0075356

Humanistic Studies in The Communication Arts

A TAXONOMY OF
CONCEPTS IN COMMUNICATION
by Reed H. Blake and Edwin O. Haroldsen

COMMUNICATIONS AND MEDIA
Constructing a Cross-Discipline
by George N. Gordon

DRAMA IN LIFE
The Uses of Communication in Society
Edited by James E. Combs and Michael W. Mansfield

Humanistic Studies in The Communication Arts

A TAXONOMY OF CONCEPTS IN COMMUNICATION

by
REED H. BLAKE
Brigham Young University
and
EDWIN O. HAROLDSEN
Brigham Young University

COMMUNICATION ARTS BOOKS

HASTINGS HOUSE, PUBLISHERS
New York 10016

LIBRARY OF CONGRESS CATALOGING IN PUBLICATION DATA
Blake, Reed H
    A taxonomy of concepts in communication.

    (Humanistic studies in the communication arts) (Commu-
nication arts books)
    Bibliography: p.
    Includes index.
    1. Communication. I. Haroldsen, Edwin O., joint
author. II. Title.
P90.B52 1975   001.5   74-34359
ISBN 0-8038-7154-6
ISBN 0-8038-7155-4 pbk.

Published simultaneously in Canada by
Saunders of Toronto, Ltd., Don Mills, Ontario

Printed in the United States of America
Designed by Al Lichtenberg

CONTENTS

Part One | Basic Elements of Communication

Part Two | Forms of Communication

Part Three | What is Communicated

Part Four | Process and Effects

Part Five | Mass Media Functions

Part Six | Social Environment for Communication

REFERENCING NOTE

To aid the reader, each concept has been given a number. This number, in boldface type, corresponds to the sequence in which the concept appears in the book. Thus *communication*, the first concept presented, is number **1**, *language* is number **2**, etc. Cross-references are included at the bottom of the first page of each concept. These refer to other concepts (and their numbers) which are felt to have close theoretical ties to the concept under review.

As an additional aid, these concept numbers are also given in parentheses in the alphabetical listing. First is the concept's number. This is followed by the series of numbers which correspond to those related concepts given at the end of the concept's discussion.

This cross-referencing system should increase the usefulness of the book.

ALPHABETICAL LISTING

TABLES

ACKNOWLEDGMENTS

The authors gratefully acknowledge the authors and publishers who gave permission to use their materials in this book.

Thomas Y. Crowell Company, Inc: From *Collective Dynamics* by Kurt Lang and Gladys Engel Lang. Copyright 1961 by Thomas Y. Crowell Company, Inc. With permission of the publishers.

The Dorsey Press: From *Sociology* by Everett K. Wilson. Copyright 1966.

Harcourt Brace Jovanovich, Inc: From *Human Behavior* by Bernard Berelson, and Gary A. Steiner. Copyright 1964 by Harcourt, Brace & World, Inc.

Harper & Row Publishers, Inc: From *Sociology* by Leonard Broom and Philip Selznick. Copyright 1955.

Hastings House Publishers: From *The War of Ideas* by George N. Gordon and Irving A. Falk. Copyright 1973. From *Communications and Media* by George N. Gordon. Copyright 1975. From *The Languages of Communication* by George N. Gordon. Copyright 1969. From *Persuasion* by George N. Gordon. Copyright 1971. From *International Communication, Media, Channels, Functions* by Heinz-Dietrich Fischer and John C. Merrill. Copyright 1970. From *The Imperative of Freedom* by John C. Merrill. Copyright 1974.

Holt, Rinehart and Winston, Inc: From *Communication and Culture* by Alfred G. Smith. Copyright 1966.

Houghton Mifflin Co: From *Interpersonal Communication: Survey and Studies* by Dean C. Barnlund (ed.). Copyright 1968.

Louisiana State University Press: From *Introduction to Mass Communications Research* by Ralph O. Nafziger and David M. White (eds.). Copyright 1958.

The Macmillan Company: From *The Complete Reporter* by Stanley Johnson and Julian Harriss. Copyright 1942. From *Survey, Design and Analysis* by Herbert Hyman. Copyright 1955. From *Towards a Sociology of Mass Communication* by Denis McQuail. Copyright 1969 by Collier-Macmillan Limited.

M.I.T. Press: From *On Human Communication* by Colin Cherry, 2nd ed. Cambridge: The M.I.T. Press, 1966.

Prentice-Hall, Inc: From *Advertising* by Maurice I. Mandell. Copyright 1968 by Prentice-Hall, Inc. From *Lesly's Public Relations Handbook* by Philip Lesly (ed.). Copyright 1971.

The Public Opinion Quarterly: From "Functional Analysis and Mass Communication" by Charles R. Wright, from *Public Opinion Quarterly*, Vol. 24, 1960.

Random House, Inc: From *The New Language of Politics* by William Safire. Copyright 1968. From *Mass Communication* by Charles R. Wright. Copyright 1959.

L. Jaganmohan Rao: "Communication Channels in the Innovation-Decision Process: Some Dimensions of Channel Concept and Tentative Hypotheses."

University of Illinois Press: From *Mass Communications* by Wilbur Schramm (ed.). Copyright 1960. From *Four Theories of the Press* by Fred S. Siebert, Theodore Peterson, and Wilbur Schramm. Copyright 1963.

Western Social Science Association: Schema from "The Relationship Between Collective Excitement and Rumor Construction," from *The Rocky Mountain Social Science Journal*, Vol. 6, 1969.

Charles R. Wright: "Partial Functional Inventory for Mass Communications." From "Functional Analysis and Mass Communication," from *Public Opinion Quarterly*, Vol. 24, 1960.

INTRODUCTION

IF THE STUDY of the communication arts and sciences suffers today from one notable systemic *Schmerz*, the malady is one of the most fashionable psychological disorders both in the therapist's clinic and on the cocktail-party circuit of instant psychoanalysis. I am referring to "identity crisis," a personality disorder usually associated with the theories of Erik Erikson who never, to my knowledge, related it directly to institutions or academic disciplines but who did indicate that this "crisis" was epidemic in our era.

I have no intention of proposing grand analytic theory in this short prologue, nor of belaboring the obvious. Let me simply note that the moment almost invariably arrives when any body of knowledge, old or new, accumulates such a dense thicket of terminology that new conceptual contributions to the field seem less important than straightening out the old ones. When that time comes, what is required to remedy the syndrome is not a psychiatrist, the therapist for personal "crises," but rather a *taxonomist*. His is the delicate problem of introducing order to apparent glut and chaos, of searching for and defining general principles among a thicket of ambiguities and classifying with parsimony apparently incompatible concepts that are actually related to one another.

For different types of intellectual endeavors, this terrible moment arrives at different times. Two thousand years intervened between Plato's suggestions for how to run the ideal school and Bloom's now-famous taxonomy of educational terminology. Closer to home, less than a generation passed between the invention and inventory of most of the gadgets that are classified and related in Rudy Bretz's recent taxonomy (compiled for the Rand Corporation) of audiovisual software and hardware. I shall not be surprised if some of our newest intellectual fields, like futurology for instance, even publish their taxonomies *before* they have in any reasonable manner structured heuristically. In fact, there may well be a taxonomical study of parapsychology or acupuncture on our bookshelves that simply has not yet come to my attention, although my name is on a lot of mailing lists.

So, for all I know, this volume, *A Taxonomy of Concepts in Com-*

munication, may be long, long overdue. I have a feeling that it is, so many and curious are the ramified rivulets into which the study of the communication arts and sciences have taken us in the past two decades. Specialized terms like "adoption curves" and "canalization" aside, how clearly do most of the men and women who teach, study and use communications research comprehend the subtle complexities of "content analysis," for instance, as fully as our best sociologists and/or psychologists understand it? (If this particular term were better or more fully understood it would not, I think, be as crudely used and abused at present by doctoral candidates, advertising researchers and pulse-takers as it is.) And what is a "rumor"? Are you prepared for the news that many, if not most, legitimate rumors on the loose at any time are quite likely to be *correct?* If not, you need a taxonomy.

Take heart, however, Most of us who consider ourselves "communications experts" of one kind or another could not clearly differentiate between *attitude* and *opinion* change if our lives hung in the balance, nor can most of the people who have to date written the best books on the subject of "attitude formation." Nor are we really able to differentiate clearly and precisely between "persuasion," "propaganda," and "information," except insofar as the word we choose in certain contexts reveals our own social and political biases. America's "propaganda" ministry is called its "information agency," and I have heard one of its gurus talking about the USIA as the United States' "public relations arm." Fine for him, but so much the worse for those of us who attempt to clarify the aims and methods that whiz around the looking-glass world of international communications.

These are not just semantic problems, as those who live with them every day know well. They are confusions of terminology that are symptoms of confusions of mind. They result, possibly inevitably, from the cross-disciplinary nature of communication study at the moment.* On the conceptual front, ideas and notions drawn from the various social and behavioral sciences (as well as the fine and popular arts) have been profusely mated one with the other to explain some of the ways that we currently use both modern technology and ancient techniques to communicate between ourselves. Just as inevitably, the time has certainly come to begin to resolve as many of these confusions judiciously and as quickly as possible.

Creating a taxonomy of anything, however, is in some measure a

---

* See my *Communications and Media: Constructing a Cross-Discipline* (cited in the Bibliography, page 149).

dangerous business because, somewhere along the way, it is bound to strip the emperor of a few of his new clothes. In the absence of taxonomical precision, one may often hide behind terminological confusions, like Moliere's physician-in-spite-of-himself, or cuddle up cozy in a miasma of vague and arbitrarily articulated concepts, secure in the knowledge that he is safe from demands for clarity or parsimony, because nobody really knows what he is talking about. In the field of communication study, we have lately been the victims of such a storm and night-fog that blew our way from Canada. Like all such airy phenomena, it drifted away bit by bit and has proven a good deal more harmless than some feared. What McLuhanism has clarified for many of us who are interested in communications, however, is the precious and pressing need we have had for a taxonomical inventory of terms and concepts about communication, whatever risks are entailed in discovering that some of our best loved assumptions actually mean less than meets the eye or are just crazy or complicated ways of stating the obvious.

To Drs. Blake and Haroldsen, then, let me extend a warm and greedy welcome to these *Humanistic Studies in the Communication Arts*. No more humane concern faces our common field of interest than the care and feeding of the language and intellectual discourse with which we must work and live. A. N. Whitehead warned us years ago to beware of *useful* books for many reasons. But I am sure that this taxonomy is an exception to his admonition. Born in the matrix of the authors' own experiences as university professors, it will, I predict, provide both a useful and fruitful set of standards for both teachers and students of communications in all their aspects, not only to resolve terminological confusions but to clarify the nature and function of the conceptual tools with which they now deal. For those of us who write about contemporary communications, this book, *A Taxonomy of Concepts in Communication,* will serve as a guidebook and lexicon that will allow us, with relief, to consign to the incinerator now obsolete bundles of file cards and notes that have been smudged and blurred from overuse in favor of its well organized lucidity.

GEORGE N. GORDON, PH.D.
Hofstra University

February 1975

PREFACE

COMMUNICATION, like sociology and geography, geology and botany, is largely a descriptive discipline. A necessary component, then, for the systematic development of communication knowledge is a body of descriptive information concerning various aspects of the field. In short, an appropriate taxonomy of concepts that encompasses this information.

The development of this taxonomy has come slowly, given the nature of communication study. That nature is that the field of communication is only now emerging into an identity of its own—for its development has been, and still largely remains today, in many separate disciplines: sociology, journalism, psychology, speech, social psychology, engineering, anthropology, among others. Still, an emerging is taking place, reflective more and more of a trend toward a dominant behavioristic approach.

As a taxonomy, this book seeks to provide simple, terse explanations of the most basic concepts in communication, and from time to time to reinforce these explanations with appropriate illustrations or other material. For the undergraduate, it seeks to stand as an introduction to these concepts; for the graduate student and others, it seeks to help broaden and systematize their work in the dynamic field of communication.

Specifically, the book provides a working shorthand for the communicator. It provides the student with a vocabulary that will enable him to express himself more easily and more clearly than is otherwise possible, thus bringing precision to his own communication.

The shorthand works this way: the student uses a term; this term functions as a label for certain objects, events, processes, etc.; these objects, events, processes, etc., are included in a concept; the term stands for this concept.

A concept is a term that describes significant common phenomena. (Most often this commonality is not self-apparent but is revealed only as someone, through mental exercise, isolates common elements.) Consequently, concepts help us organize and understand the events at hand. Concept building (isolating those aspects that explain behavior) is at the center core of communication research and study.

A concept, then, is a symbol of the things or phenomena we are studying. It is a term referring to common elements or qualities. Thus, the concept "news" is not a specific news story, but the term including the essential qualities found in all news stories—qualities such as perishability, interest to a particular audience, new information, information urgently needed. Using a concept such as "news" helps us deal with a mass of details, to abstract commonalities from them. It also guides us in what to look for when we are seeking answers to particular problems. For example, the concept "news" might help a researcher seeking to compare the performance of two newspapers.

As has been noted, each concept has a term (label, name) that describes it, such as "news." This name can stand in place of the concept. "Nothing," says Bain (1964: 77),* "can be observed as a datum for science that cannot be named or categorized; hence, all observations require symbols and concepts . . ." From this point, the communications investigator is able to engage in theory construction. As Merton (1957: 89) has observed:

> It is only when such concepts are interrelated in the form of a scheme that a theory begins to emerge. Concepts, then, constitute the definitions (or prescriptions) of what is to be observed; they are the variables between which empirical relationships are to be sought. When propositions are logically interrelated, a theory has been instituted.

The concepts treated here were selected by the authors for their usefulness in understanding the process and effects of communication. Not all the concepts used by the communicator are included, but the major ones are. They are heavily reflective of the behavioral approach to communication. This is viewed as a strength, for such concepts have advanced the field beyond the superficiality that marked the earlier years of communication endeavors. Like other scientific undertakings, prediction should be the goal of our field, as well.

The book is divided into seven parts, which, in a broad sense, reflect the authors' approach to the book's construction. *Part One* deals with those concepts we saw as Basic (or key) Elements in the Approach to Communication. In the book's preparation, we called these concepts in such a manner, and so put it as the title of *Part One*. This section begins with a treatment of the concept on which this taxonomy is built, that of communication. It is followed by the

---

* Author references (copyright date and page number) are to books cited in the Bibliography, see page 147.

concept of language, the basic carrier of communication, and its basic component, the symbol. This is followed by a discussion on those who participate in communication, the sender and receiver, and what they transmit, the message. In turn, the problems besetting all types of communication—communication noise—is then treated, followed by the way in which communication is made, the channel, and then the major categories of channel, informal and formal. The section concludes with a discussion on communication networks.

Part Two is headed Communication Forms. It begins with the communication form of intrapersonal communication, an individual activity, and ends with political communication, a very collective process. Between these two concepts are eight others, which suggests the range of the field.

Part Three centers on What is Communicated. It contains discussions on the nature of news, editorializing, objective journalism, advertising, publicity, public relations, and propaganda.

Part Four concerns itself with what we call Process and Effects of Communication, and includes socialization, attitude and opinion, attitude change, selective exposure, perception, and retention, and communicator's intent.

Part Five treats what is popularly referred to as Functions of the Mass Media. (We should add, however, that many of the concepts in this section are useful in the analysis of other forms of communication.) The section is based on the integrative work of Charles R. Wright.

In *Part Six* are presented those concepts concerning the Social Environment for Communication; that is to say, the communication setting and the social forces involved. Eight concepts are handled.

Part Seven, to conclude the book, handles those concepts viewed as contributing to Investigative Approaches and Tools. Twelve concepts are discussed.

To all who helped in the preparation and publication of this book, we offer our heartfelt thanks. Particularly, we owe a debt of gratitude to George N. Gordon for his many helpful comments on the manuscript; also to Gordon Whiting for providing the framework for the discussion on traditions in communication research; and to Wayne Pace, Brent Peterson, Dallas Burnett, Gary Bunker, and John Seggar for their suggestions on selected parts of the manuscript while it was in progress.

REED H. BLAKE
EDWIN O. HAROLDSEN

February 1975

Part One

BASIC ELEMENTS
OF COMMUNICATION

1 | COMMUNICATION

OUR ABILITY to communicate and the forms of the communication are all too often taken for granted, report Hartley and Hartley (1961: 18, 33). "The communication process is the basis of all that we call social in the functioning of the living organism. In man, it is essential to the development of the individual, to the formation and continued existence of groups, and to the interrelations among groups." The Hartleys label communication the *basic social process.*

What, then, is communication? Gerbner (1958) defines communication as social interaction through messages—messages that can be formally coded, symbolic, or representational events of some shared aspect of a culture. One of the more widely used definitions is:

> The transmission of information, ideas, emotions, skills, etc., by use of symbols—words, pictures, figures, graphs, etc. It is the *act* or *process* of transmission that is usually called communication. (Berelson and Steiner, 1964:527.)

As process, communication is at once specific and general, narrow and broad in its scope:

> Human communication is a subtle and ingenious set of processes. It is always thick with a thousand ingredients—signals, codes, meanings—no matter how simple the message or the transaction. Human communication is also a varied set of processes. It can use any one of a hundred different means, either words or gestures or punched cards, either intimate conversations or mass media and world-wide audiences. . . . Whenever people interact, they communicate. . . . When people control one another, they do so primarily through communication. (Smith, 1966:v.)

While communication is a widely used concept, one must emphasize that there is not complete agreement among observers as to the dimensions of the term. Some hold that there is no communication unless the receiver of a message is affected by it. Others such as Miller (1966) insist that the study of communications prop-

2 | Language.   3 | Symbol.   5 | Message.

erly should focus only on situations in which a source transmits a message to a receiver with a *conscious intent to affect the latter's behavior*. Thus, he apparently would not consider the field of communication to include situations in which meaning is unconsciously conveyed by one to another. The political candidate who absent mindedly jaywalks, in Miller's view, is technically not communicating—though he may have conveyed an unintended impression and inadvertently influenced those who saw him.

For the individual, communication performs three major functions.

1. Communication patterns the world for the individual.
2. Communication defines the individual's own position in relation to other people.
3. Communication helps the individual adapt successfully to his environment. (Hartley and Hartley, 1961:19.)

A central concern of the study of communication is the production, organization, composition, structure, distribution, historical development, and functions of message systems in society (Gerbner, 1958). Three major approaches to the study of the communication process have made the most empirical contribution to the field, says Smith (1966). They are (1) mathematical, (2) social psychological, and (3) linguistic-anthropological (Smith, 1966).

The accompanying typology illustrates these major approaches. It is a synthesis and adaptation of the integrative approach taken by Smith in his book, *Communication and Culture*. Smith further suggests that here communication investigators are concerned with three basic areas: syntactic, semantic, and pragmatic.

APPROACHES TO THE STUDY OF HUMAN COMMUNICATION

	Investigator	Source of Interest	Key Orientation	Major Area of Concern
Mathematical:	Electronic engineers Theoretical physicists Communication analysts	Technical developments in telecommunications engineering	Analysis of information in terms of probability and statistics	Syntactics: within messages Semantics: no concern Pragmatics: no concern
Social Psychology:	Social and behavioral scientists	Study of group dynamics	Analysis of human codes and networks	Syntactics: Between messages Semantics: Cultural aspects of coding and decoding symbols Pragmatics: How people react to decoded symbols
Linguistic Anthropology:	Linguists Anthropologists	Cross-cultural comparisons of human behavior	Analysis of speech	Syntactics: Within messages Semantics: Cultural aspects of coding and decoding symbols Pragmatics: Little concern

Syntactics is concerned with the relations of symbols to symbols.

Semantics is concerned with the meaning of messages.

Pragmatics is concerned with relations between signals and their effects on people.

2 | LANGUAGE

LANGUAGE IS A system of symbols—oral and written—used by members of a social community in a fairly standardized way to call forth meaning. As Hollander (1967) observes, language is the "strikingly distinctive attribute of Man." It is acquired from contact with other human beings and consists of symbolized meanings which act as sources of stimulation and mediators of responses.

> Every human group that anthropologists have studied has spoken a language. The language always has a lexicon and a grammar. The lexicon is not a haphazard collection of vocalizations, but is highly organized; it always has pronouns, means for dealing with time, space, and number, words to represent true and false, the basic concepts necessary to propositional logic. The grammar has distinguishable levels of structure, some phonological, some syntactic. . . . The syntax always specifies rules for grouping elements sequentially into phrases and sentences, rules governing normal intonation, rules for transforming some types of sentences into other types (Miller, 1964:34).

Krech, et al. (1962) feel that it would be difficult indeed to overstate the importance of language in the affairs of man. They give to language three major functions:

1. Language is the primary vehicle for communication.

2. Language reflects both the personality of the individual and the culture of his society. In turn it helps shape both personality and culture.

3. Language makes possible the growth and transmission of culture, the continuity of societies, and the effective functioning and control of social groups.

1 | Communication. 3 | Symbol.

3 | SYMBOL

A SYMBOL is something used deliberately to stand for something else. What it stands for is what the social group says it stands for. There is no necessary relation between the symbol and the thing for which it stands, that is, the "referent." As society agrees that a given symbol stands for a particular object, members of the society tend to see the symbol and object as inseparable. Thus, *horse* (in verbal, written, or gestural form) becomes the proper way to refer to a particular animal. Consequently, if an individual uses some other word—as symbol, for instance—to stand for such an animal, it will most often result in blocked communication. Consequently, the world in which man lives is a world of symbols.

A major characteristic of symbols, notes Hoebel (1966:299), is their non-diffuseness:

> In one form or another, symbols are always overt; they must be seen, heard, felt, or smelled. They condense abstractions into delimited objects.

The great gulf that separates man from other forms of animals is that man, and man alone, engages in symbolic interaction. Further, man himself creates the symbols he uses. When the symbols that men use to communicate—vocalizations, written words, gestures, etc.—go beyond a normal range of shared meanings and elicit the same, or nearly the same, responses in both sender and receiver, such a symbol(s) is called a *significant symbol.*

Symbols, then, are the basic units of communication systems. They can be verbal, as in the spoken word; graphic, as in the written word; or representational, as in flag, banner, etc.

1 | Communication. 2 | Language. 5 | Message. 27 | Socialization.

4 | SENDER / RECEIVER

THE BASIC model for understanding the communication process has been Lasswell's (1948) paradigm of who says what, in which channel, to whom, with what effect (source: message: channel: receiver: effect). In this discussion, we are concerned with the "who" and the "whom"—the actors in the communication drama.

Traditionally, this area of study has been called *control analysis* (the who) and *audience analysis* (the whom).

There are a number of labels that have been posited to describe this relationship. Among others—and in various combinations—they include:

(stimulus)	—	(response)
sender		receiver
encoder		decoder
source		destination
actor		audience
communicator		communicatee

All of the above point to the notion that to have communication there must be two or more actors involved—that a message must be sent, but also that it must be received. The left-hand column (sender, encoder, etc.) represents the agent who plays the part of initiating and guiding the act of communication. The right-hand column represents those participants who, by their reception of the message (of whatever dimension), permit the communicative act to be completed, to have some kind of effect. Without both actors, communication cannot occur. Further, both actors must share the same "social environment" so that the symbols used have common meaning.

Some communication analysts make a further distinction between the encoder-decoder and the other paired statuses listed earlier. Berlo (1960:30) says:

> The communication encoder is responsible for taking the ideas of the source and putting them into a code, expressing the source's purpose in the form of a message. . . .

3 | Symbol.   5 | Message.   51 | Two-Step Flow Theory.

8

Just as a source needs an encoder . . . the receiver needs a decoder to retranslate, to decode the message and put it into a form that the receiver can use.

From this perspective, the basic communication model now looks like this: source: encoder: message: channel: decoder: receiver: effect.

Still, whether or not the source acts as his own encoder (as in the case of most oral communication) and whether or not the receiver acts as his own decoder (again in most oral communication), the central aspect with the former is stimulus control—initiating and guiding; and the central aspect of the latter is response—reception behavior.

5 | MESSAGE

IN THE LASSWELL (1948) communication model of

Who
Says What
In Which Channel
To Whom
With What Effect?

the "says what" is the message. A message is an ordered selection of symbols intended to communicate information. By ordered, we mean a deliberate arrangement. By selection, we mean the making of a discrimination from a larger set of alternatives.

Specialists who focus upon the "says what" engage in what is called *content analysis*. However, such specialists are concerning themselves more and more with the total message and not just its content. By content, we mean the meaning of a message.

Often message (as in the harsh statement, "Get the message?") is used interchangeably with content. In the field of communication the two are not the same. Content is one aspect of message. Berlo (1960:54) lists three major message factors: (1) the message code, (2) the message content, and (3) the message treatment.

Message code has to do with the way in which symbols are structured. Content has to do with selection of material to express a purpose. Treatment has to do with the way in which the message is presented, that is, frequency, redundancy, emphasis, etc.

Another dimension of message is that of message-production activities (such as length) and message-handling activities (such as placement).

That which a message receives from its audience is called message *exposure:* the act of receiving (reading, listening, viewing) mes-

1 | Communication. 2 | Language. 3 | Symbol. 6 | Communication Noise. 21 | News. 22 | Editorial/Editorializing. 23 | Objective Journalism. 24 | Advertising/Publicity. 25 | Public Relations. 26 | Propaganda.

sages, passively or actively. Usually, however, active reception of the message is called *attention*.

Messages, then, are sets of symbols—most often language—in the transmission of meaning from sender to receiver.

6 | COMMUNICATION NOISE

BOTH FORMAL and informal communication channels are subject to "noise," the ultimate limiter of effective message transmission. There are two major types of communication noise—channel and semantic. In either case, the result of the noise is the same—the loss of meaning during the transmission.

Channel noise. This type of noise includes any disturbance which interferes with the fidelity of the physical transmission of the message (Emery, Ault, Agee, 1965). In mass communication, channel noise includes such diverse disturbances as static on the radio, smeared ink in the newspaper, a rolling screen in television, or type too small to read in a magazine. Emery also includes as channel noise "all distractions between source and audience."

In interpersonal communication, someone speaking in a room over another conversation, a door shutting, and other such distractions can also be considered channel noise, since the distraction impairs the transfer of information. "Cross-talk" often heard during long-distance telephone calls is an example of noise in medio communication.

Semantic noise. This type of noise results in the wrong interpretation of messages (Cherry, 1966). Within any type of communication activity there often is a discrepancy between the codes used by the encoder and the decoder, even though the message is received exactly as it was sent (Bush, 1954).

Communication researchers cite the following as sources of semantic noise:

1. Words too difficult, subject too difficult, etc., for the message receiver to grasp.

2. Differences in selected denotative meaning of word(s) between the message sender and receiver—i.e., message receiver thinking that the word points to something different than that intended by the sender.

3. Differences in connotative meaning of word(s) between message sender and receiver—i.e., differences in meanings which they associate with the word.

1 | Communication. 2 | Language. 3 | Symbol. 5 | Message.

4. A sentence pattern confusing to the message receiver.

5. A message organization pattern confusing to the message receiver.

6. Cultural differences between message sender and message receiver—i.e., intonation, use of eyes, hands or other body movements.

COMMUNICATION NOISE

Channel Noise

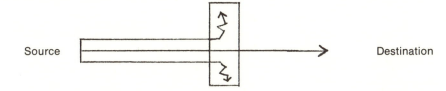

Source → Destination

After being placed in a channel, the message is interfered with by some disturbance, which (1) increased the difficulty in reception or (2) prevented some elements of the message from reaching its destination, or both.

Semantic Noise

Source → Destination

Elements of the message itself are not understood by the receiver, and, hence, are filtered out (lost to the receiver). The result is that the full intended meaning does not reach its destination.

7 | COMMUNICATION CHANNEL

A COMMUNICATION channel is the medium utilized to convey a message. It is the avenue or means by which a message travels between the communicator (source or sender) and the communicatee (receiver).

> Communication channels are the effective links inter-connecting the source-receiver nodes in a communication structure, through which messages flow. Channels couple the source and the receiver, enabling them to communicate. Channel thus is a fertile concept with constitutive linkages to other concepts like source, receiver, and message in communication theory. (Rao, 1972:4.)

The communication channel, Rao suggests, is distinguished by the following characteristics:

1. It is a type of matter-energy unit, called a medium.
2. It carries some patterned matter-energy units, called information.
3. It is a coupling mechanism or link between participating units in communication.

He also suggests that communication channels have "dimensions." These dimensions permit the investigator to evaluate the relative effectiveness of different communication channels. These dimensions include:

Channel credibility. The expertness and trustworthiness of a channel as perceived by the receivers. Often channel credibility is directly linked to communicator and audience characteristics. In general, however, print media are perceived by members of upper socio-economic groupings as being more credible; television is perceived as more credible by lower socio-economic groupings.

Channel feedback. The opportunity a channel provides for the

5 | Message. 8 | Informal Channels of Communications. 9 | Formal Channels of Communication. 11 | Intrapersonal Communication. 12| Interpersonal Communication. 15 | Medio Communication. 16 | Mass Communication.

receiver to respond immediately and maximally to affect the source of the message in a communication transaction. Face-to-face communication tends to facilitate feedback; mass communication tends to restrict it.

Channel involvement (or participation). The perceptual effort required by all the senses in order to comprehend information from a communication channel. Here again, face-to-face communication offers the greatest possibility for involvement; print media the least possibility for involvement.

Channel availability. The frequency and extent to which a channel may be used to reach a given audience. In some geographic areas, some channels may not be available, such as television in sparsely populated areas, or print media in highly illiterate areas.

Channel permanency (or ability to preserve a message). The durability of a communication channel over time to carry the message. Print media have this dimension to a large degree; by contrast, radio does not.

Channel multiplicative power. The channel's relative potential for covering an extensive geographical area with speed and timeliness. The mass media can multiply a message and make it available to large numbers of people simultaneously; face-to-face communication is low on this dimension.

Channel complementarity. The channel's potential for supplementing the communication work of another channel. Both mass media and interpersonal channels have proven to be high on this dimension.

8 | INFORMAL CHANNELS OF COMMUNICATION

INFORMAL CHANNELS of communication are interpersonal communication networks built up around face-to-face interaction of persons with common interests or purposes. Over time, these networks tend to become highly stable and reliable sources of information.

There are two major types of informal channels:

1. The spontaneously formed channel. This is a message interchange in an unstructured network made up of people who for the most part are largely unaware of each other's identity and station in life. This kind of channel is most used in public places or in times of high collective excitement when participants feel the need and/or freedom to exchange information with relatively unknown persons.

2. The auxiliary channels. This is a message interchange in networks built around personal friendships and purposes which bring people together.

> The roles enacted in auxiliary channels are not fixed in custom nor defined in law. These sources are evaluated largely in terms of personal reputation of the participants for honesty, knowledge, sound judgment, and "connections." (Shibutani, 1966:23.)

It is in auxiliary channels that most interpersonal communication takes place.

A characteristic of the interpersonal network is the passage of information whose content is for the most part nowhere fixed and verified. Rather, those in the informal networks are not held accountable for the content of the message, but merely for its transmission (more so in the spontaneously formed channels than in auxiliary channels). Thus, members of the informal channels are participants in two roles: they are recipients of information and they are transmitters of information. Lang and Lang (1967) have labeled these people *recipient-transmitters.*

News that is disseminated by informal channels is known as *informal news* and as *unverified news*.

Under normal conditions, a given person's interpersonal networks vary from situation to situation. In a given situation interpersonal networks vary from person to person. An investigator can only look at an interpersonal network in terms of *one* participant and *one* topic to determine the boundaries of that network. For instance, A's network has boundaries peculiar to A. B, C, and D may constitute A's standard network in, say, the area of sports. But B's network in this area may include A, E, G, and H—none of whom are part of A's network.

Central communicators. Within any interpersonal network, the rate of message interchange is not equal among all participants. Indeed, in any network, some people enjoy a higher rate of participant contact than do others.

This higher contact may be due to the fact that the individual occupies certain social positions; it may be due to the fact that certain psychological factors peculiar to the individual himself are at play; or it may be due to both factors. Berlo (1960:48) notes that some people hold positions in society that are communication-prone. "These include receptionists, salesmen, barbers, elected politicians, waitresses: people whose role-behavior increase their contact with others." On the other hand, many people (irrespective of their social positions) may enact these central communication roles as a way of fulfilling certain psychological wants, such as the desire for attention, to be needed, and the like.

To a degree, the rate of message interchange also may be due to physical factors. For example, a secretary located near the boss's office may be involved in more conversations than a secretary of equal status at another desk.

Central communicators, then, are people who for whatever reason have a higher than average rate of message interchange in informal communication networks.

A COMPARISON OF FORMAL AND INFORMAL CHANNELS
OF COMMUNICATION

	Channel	*Participant*	*News*	*Source*

INFORMAL	Auxiliary
	  Interpersonal networks
	  Rumor systems
	  Spontaneous
		Recipient-
		  transmitters
			Informal
			  and
			Unverified
				Often fugitive

FORMAL	Institutional
	  Mass media
	  Official meetings and
	    gatherings
	  Organizational networks
		Professional
		  personnel
		Officers
			Formal
			  and
			Verified
				Identifiable

9 | FORMAL CHANNELS OF COMMUNICATION

THE DISTINGUISHING characteristic of a formal channel of communication, as Shibutani (1966) notes, is that it is authoritative, that it serves as the standard against which reports attributed to all other sources are checked.

Within an organization, formal channels "represent the 'official' lines of communication—those designated on organization charts and specified in position descriptions" (Redding and Sanborn, 1964:46). On a society-wide basis, the formal channels are basically equated with the mass media (Shibutani, 1966:20–21). The important matter, then, is not whether the communication occurs through personal contact, print, or some electronic device. Rather, it is whether the channel itself is defined as authoritative.

A second characteristic is that within the channel the message source can be identified. For example, in formal communication via the mass media, the news source is identifiable and, hence, accountable. As Lang and Lang (1967:60) assert, "Editors and commentators can never extricate themselves from the responsibility for evaluating the news they pass on." The information that is passed on thus has the "seal of approval of the entire news organization, which must always face the possibility of libel suits."

Formal channels of communication are well organized channels:

> Like other social institutions they are characterized by a stable set of rules, officers performing clearly defined roles, procedures so well established as to be followed by interchangeable personnel, and sustaining sanctions. There are fixed standards of acceptability, prescribed routes of transmission, verification procedures, and codes of reliable conduct. Since the participants are readily identifiable, they are held personally accountable for their performance.

The fixing of responsibility, considerations of personal pride, and concern over one's reputation within the organization tend to temper the pursuit of personal predilections at the expense of accurate communication. (Shibutani, 1966:21.)

Formal channels are also known as institutional channels.

News that is disseminated by formal channels is known as formal news and as verified news.

CHARACTERISTICS OF FORMAL CHANNELS IN MASS AND TRADITIONAL SOCIETIES

Communication Elements	Mass Society	Traditional Society
Channel	Media (Broadcast)	Oral (Point-to-point)
Audience	Mass (Heterogeneous)	Primary (Homogeneous)
Source	Professional (Skill)	Hierarchical (Status)
Content	Mainly descriptive	Mainly perscriptive

The nature of the formal channels of communication varies according to the type of society in which the channels function. This point is illustrated in the schema above, which compares the formal channels in a mass society with the formal channels in a traditional society. Adapted from Daniel Lerner, 1960.

10 | COMMUNICATION NETWORK

THE TERM communication network designates a system for the dissemination of information among the members of a group.

Communication networks can be viewed as one of two major types, informal or formal. Informal networks are often referred to as *emergent communication networks*. These networks occur in interpersonal communication in which no one consciously assigns or enforces the use of specific points of contact. Rather, the networks "emerge" as participants freely interact with anyone, in differing rates of intensity and frequency. Studies have indicated that over time, these emergent networks tend to become stable and reliable sources of information. Rumor, gossip, and other unstructured forms of information exchange are the basic types of transactions in these networks.

Formal networks are often referred to as *prescribed communication networks*. These networks are a type of interpersonal communication in which the interaction occurs in deliberately designed networks. Thus, these networks are structured. In the structuring process, status-roles are major considerations. Much social life today requires the patterning of communicative networks.

Both types of networks have *net connectivity:* the degree to which a participant has communication access to other members of the network. In the "all-channel" net, all members have access to one another. In the "restricted" net, some of the participants have limited or no access at all to some members of the network.

8 | Informal Channels of Communication. 9 | Formal Channels of Communication.

Part Two

FORMS OF COMMUNICATION

11 | INTRAPERSONAL COMMUNICATION

INTRAPERSONAL COMMUNICATION is a communication transaction that takes place within the individual. In short, it is talking to oneself.

Intrapersonal communication is made possible because man can become object to himself through the use of the symbols used in his communication. Through these symbols what man "says to others can mean the same to himself as it does to them" (Duncan, 1962:76).

While all communication is to some extent intrapersonal communication—that is, the meanings involved in every communication are always subject to our own private interpretation—the concept of intrapersonal communication as a distinct concept is useful to many students of this aspect of the broader topic:

> The encoding-decoding process that occurs while a man waits alone outside an operating room or introspects about some personal tragedy is a sufficiently distinctive type of communication to require separate analysis. For this reason it is desirable to restrict "intrapersonal communication" to the manipulation of cues within an individual that occurs in the absence of other people (although they may be symbolically present in the imagination). As such, its locus is confined to a single person transacting with his environment. He sees what his purposes require, senses what his organism will admit, associates signs according to the dynamics of his own personality. (Barnlund, 1968:8.)

This distinction permits intrapersonal communication to be ordered along a continuum of communication types that include intrapersonal, interpersonal, medio, and mass communication.

12 | INTERPERSONAL COMMUNICATION

INTERPERSONAL COMMUNICATION is direct communication between two or more people in physical proximity in which all of the five senses can be utilized and immediate feedback is present.

One of the more widely used conceptualizations, an adaption on Hovland (1948:371), defines interpersonal communication as an interacting situation in which an individual (the communicator) transmits stimuli (usually verbal symbols) to modify the behavior of other individuals (communicatees), in a face-to-face setting.

More recently, Barnlund (1968:8–10) has identified five characteristics of this type of communicative activity:

1. Initially, there is a "perceptual engagement" on the part of two or more people in physical proximity. While an incomplete basis for interpersonal communication, this "sort of rudimentary social contact is prerequisite to [this type activity]."

2. Perceptual engagement provides the communicative interdependence that allows for focused interaction—a single focus of cognitive and visual attention, as in a conversation. In focused interaction each participant supplies cues in direct response to the cues supplied by the other participant(s).

3. This focused interaction proceeds through an exchange of messages. In this exchange the participants present to each other cues they think the other will interpret as intended, cues which will convey the intended message to the other.

4. The interaction is on a face-to-face basis. Hence, all of the senses may be exploited, and participants can confront each other totally.

5. Finally, the interpersonal setting is largely unstructured; few rules govern the frequency, form, or content of interpersonal messages.

In summary, Barnlund says, the study of interpersonal communication is concerned with the investigation of relatively informal social situations in which persons in face-to-face encounters sustain a focused interaction through the reciprocal exchange of verbal and nonverbal cues.

13 | ORGANIZATIONAL COMMUNICATION

ORGANIZATIONAL COMMUNICATION is a form of interpersonal communication, but its characteristics are such as to constitute a distinctive and significant area of study.

Organizational communication has, to begin with, the dominant characteristics of interpersonal communication: it involves face-to-face, focused interaction; it makes use of all of the senses; it provides immediate feedback. However, organizational communication is also marked by number and status-role considerations, such as role prescriptions, professional norms, prescribed routes of transmission, sanctions, and the like.

In contrast to the larger area of interpersonal communication, organizational communication boundaries are more sharply defined, less permeable. In a general focused interacting situation one may be hardly aware of whether he is "in" or "out." But he is usually quite aware of his membership in an organization. If he's excluded from an organization altogether, he cannot communicate as a member. If he's included he is obligated to communicate in certain prescribed ways.

Though organizations vary in size, permanence, and tasks to be performed, they all have members interacting with each other, occupying various social positions, and playing social roles. Some patterns of action are rewarded and reinforced by the organization's members. Other patterns are stifled through disapproval. Thus norms of appropriate behavior evolve and provide group members with standards for assessing the appropriateness of communicative acts. Communication in an organization becomes fairly predictable with regard to the direction, frequency, form, and even content of the messages exchanged (Barnlund, 1968:10–11).

A final characteristic of organizational communication is the serial reproduction of messages. In this kind of reproduction, mes-

9 | Formal Channels of Communication. 10 | Communication Network. 12 | Interpersonal Communication. 46 | Gatekeeper.

sages are transmitted from one person to another, then from that person to still another, and so on. But each communications act remains predominately a dyadic or two-person interaction.

The major transmission form in organizational communication is oral. However, print, in the form of memos, punched cards, etc., is frequently employed. But in final analysis these forms are auxiliary to the face-to-face encounters, or its substitutes (as the telephone). In a broader sense, too, the study of organizational communication must take into account the "shadow channels"—the informal channels of organizations. Like a shadow, the informal channel is an ever-present approximation of the formal organization, dispensing its own information and acting as a feedback mechanism. It can in some instances be a useful (functional) adjunct to the organization; it can also be a harmful (dysfunctional) one.

While the characteristics of organizational communication and formal channels are much alike, the two should not be confused. Organizational communication is basically concerned with the dissemination of information to members of the group, including the forms this dissemination takes. It is a *type* of communication activity. The criteria of a formal, as opposed to an informal, channel is whether or not the communication is authoritative. Here the focus is on the *nature* of the message.

The official routes of organizational communication are formal channels of communication. But formal channels are not limited to organizations. Formal channels serve not only organizations but also audiences and publics as well.

In summary, organizational communication is communication that takes place within definite boundaries and is concerned with the achievement of the goals of that organization.

14 | RUMOR

RUMOR IS A widespread report from an unknown source.

It is a collective transaction whose component parts consist of intellectual and communicative activity; it develops as men caught together in an ambiguous situation attempt to construct a meaningful interpretation of the situation by pooling their intellectual resources (Shibutani, 1966:164).

In short, rumor is a collective effort to find a definition (Lang and Lang, 1967).

Both the formal and informal channels of communication are important elements in the rumor process. As a collective transaction, rumor develops in the informal (interpersonal) channels. As Lang and Lang (1967:53) note, the networks through which rumor travels may be described as fugitive:

> . . . the paths seem to elude us as we try to track down a rumor. Even though the rumor content itself becomes public knowledge and displaces or supplants official information, the channels themselves are never public or official.

While its transmission is through the informal channels, rumor is a result of insufficient information from the formal channels.

> Rumor is a substitute for [verified] news; in fact, it is news that does not develop in institutional channels. Unsatisfied demand for news—the discrepancy between information needed to come to terms with a changing environment and what is provided by formal news channels—constitutes the crucial condition of rumor construction. (Shibutani, 1966:62.)

Of importance in the study of rumor is the fact that truth is not a criterion. In fact, because rumor is both communicative and cognitive activity, most rumors are true.

Gossip. Like rumor, gossip is unverified news that is transmitted through the interpersonal channels. The basic difference between

8 | Informal Channels of Communication.   10 | Communication Network.   12 | Interpersonal Communication.   47 | Collective Excitement.

30

the two is that gossip is news of interest within the confines of a "neighborhood," while rumor is news of interest beyond those confines.

> Gossip is restricted to small local groups in which members are bound in personal contacts and concerns the private and intimate details of the traits and conduct of specific individuals. (Shibutani, 1966:41.)

Most gossip is local in nature, dealing largely with deviations of the moral code. It is a powerful mechanism for social control; consequently, much of what people do and don't do is a result of gossip or the fear of gossip.

15 | MEDIO COMMUNICATION

TRADITIONALLY, the communication process has been divided into two broad categories: interpersonal and mass communication. More recently, however, as communication interest and research increased, surveys of the full range of communication activity disclosed that the traditional dichotomy did not encompass all types of communication, that much ongoing communication activity could not be classified into either of the standard categories.

What emerged was a third area of study, medio communication, which concerns itself with that area of communication activity which lies in the interface between face-to-face and mass communication.

Medio communication is distinguished by the presence of a technical instrument which is most often used under restricted conditions involving identifiable participants. It is, then, an intermediate level of communication (medio: from the Latin meaning middle) that has characteristics of both interpersonal and mass communication.

Like interpersonal communication, the recipient of the message in medio communication is normally small in number—often only one—and is known to the communicator. The message is most often transmitted under restricted conditions (hence the message is not public). The participants usually enjoy an intellectual mutuality most often associated with interpersonal communication. And, finally, the interaction pattern, to a fair degree, is unstructured.

On the other hand, as in mass communication situations, members of a medio communication audience can be heterogeneous and can be widely separated from each other in space—i.e. receive the same message in different physical locations. The message is transmitted rapidly, reaching most audience members simultaneously. The communicator may or may not operate within a complex organization, but the channel he utilizes most often is expensive. Finally, as in mass communication, a distinguishing characteristic of medio communication is the presence of a technical instrument for message transmission.

Medio communication includes point-to-point telecommunications (telephone, teletype, mobile radio, air-to-ground radio, etc.), surveilance telecommunication (radar, atmospheric pollution monitoring, weather satellite, etc.), closed-circuit television (industrial, education, etc.), and home movies, among others.

16 | MASS COMMUNICATION

MASS COMMUNICATION is a process. And although modern technology in the form of the mass media is essential to the process, the presence of these technical instruments should not be mistaken for the process itself. Mass communication, as identified by Wright (1959), is distinguished by the following characteristics.

1. It is directed toward relatively large, heterogeneous, and anonymous audiences.

2. Messages are transmitted publicly, often timed to reach most audience members simultaneously, and are transient in character.

3. The communicator tends to be, or to operate within, a complex organization that may involve great expense.

At any given time thousands of people under quasi-isolated and impersonal conditions receive common stimuli. In this way they are admitted to a kind and range of social experience that lie outside the orbit of ordinary social life and primary communication: the mass communication process defines and allocates the categorical roles of communicator (source) and communicatee (receiver); it reduces or eliminates the dimension of interpersonal relations in the process of communication; it tends to detach individuals from their traditional socio-cultural surroundings; and it extends the horizons of life at a level and in a realm beyond that of ordinary social action (Himes, 1968:378–380).

Every mass-communicated act can be broken down into five elements: *communicators* who transmit a given *message* through a *channel* to an *audience* with some kind of *effect*. The definition of mass communication touches only the first four elements; yet it is the effects of mass communication that concern most people in the world today.

The following schema will aid the student in understanding the

9 | Formal Channels of Communication. 17 | Mass Media. 21 | News. 22 | Editorial/Editorializing.   23 | Objective Journalism.   24 | Advertising/Publicity.   25 | Public Relations.   26 | Propaganda. 32 | Mass Communication Activities.   46 | Gatekeeper.   48 | Mass Society/Mass Culture. 51 | Two-Step Flow Theory.

three major types of communication of interpersonal, medio, and mass and the relationship between them. The characteristics are not necessarily always present nor exclusive, but they do tend to appear as indicated.

CHARACTERISTICS OF INTERPERSONAL, MEDIO,

	Audience	Message	Source
Interpersonal Communication	Small number Homogeneous Identifiable Spacial proximity	Transmitted under private or restricted conditions Content has no to limited restrictions Speed of transmission determined only by normal barriers to social intercourse	Communicator often works independently of any organization No expense involved Evidence of opinion leaders
Medio Communication	Small number Heterogeneous/ homogeneous Spacial proximity and spacial distance Identifiable	Transmitted under private or restricted conditions Content is specialized and/or technical Intellectual mutuality Transmitted rapidly	Involves a degree of expense Status and professional
Mass Communication	Large number Heterogeneous Anonymous Spacial distance	Transmitted publicly Transmitted rapidly Transient in character Content is nontechnical Subject to restrictions	Communicator works through complex organization Involves a degree of expense

AND MASS COMMUNICATION

Channel	Interaction Pattern	Social Context	Sample Conditions
Informal (interpersonal)	Normally unstructured (episodic, impulsive, fragmentary) Immediate feedback	Primary	Individual face-to-face dialogue Family discussions Club meetings
Informal and Formal	Can be highly structured or unstructured Can be immediate or delayed	Primary-secondary	Individual to individual dialogue via intermediary device such as telephone Ship-to-shore messages Classes taught via closed-circuit television
Formal (mass media)	Structured Feedback delayed	Secondary	Commercial television, newspapers, radio, magazines, etc. Skywriting Billboards Direct mail campaigns

17 | MASS MEDIA

THE TERM "mass media" often is applied to the technical devices through which mass communication takes place. From this point of view, the mass media may be considered to include:

1. *Print media*—newspapers, magazines, books, pamphlets, direct mail circulars, billboards, skywriting, and any other technical device that carries a message to the masses by appealing to the sense of sight.

2. *Electronic media*—(a) radio programs and audio recordings that appeal to the sense of sound, (b) television programs, motion pictures and video recordings that appeal to both the sense of sound and sense of sight.

A mass medium can be conceptualized as operating in one of three levels in terms of its impact on mass society. For instance, in the United States, on the first level are the four major mass media—newspapers, magazines, radio, and television.

On the second—or intermediate—level are books and motion pictures. These two media were once major forces in our society; while they still have great impact, they probably do not affect as high a percentage of society as in past decades.

On the third—or minor—level are the remaining media, such as billboards, direct mail and the like.

It is not the instrument itself but the way it is used that differentiates a mass medium from a limited medium. To qualify as a mass medium, the technical instrument must not only (1) offer the possibility of communication via a mechanical device, making for an impersonal relationship between the communicator and his audience, but it must also (2) actually be used to communicate from a single source to a large (mass) number of persons. Thus, home movies are not a mass medium.

In a mass society, the mass media are considered sources of verified news. Thus, while the news disseminated by those who work within the complex organization known as the mass media may, in fact, be false, what is central is that the report can still be traced to its source. To a large extent, this ensures society, under threat of disclosure, that reports will tend to be truthful—or that with the audience members knowing the source, they can identify certain biases (attempts to manipulate others) or censorship in the reports.

The mass media are a relatively new social phenomenon, just a few hundred years old. The advent of the media required two developments: (1) a relatively advanced technology to produce the necessary instruments, and (2) an accompanying level of literacy among large numbers of people to utilize the disseminated information. But the mass media both depend on and affect human literacy and education. Moreover, within the limits of free time the human appetite for all mass media appears to rise with education (Schramm, 1973:182).

Today the mass media are pervasive in the United States. Radios are found in 98% of homes, television sets in 93%; 90% of American adults see a daily newspaper regularly, 60 to 70% of adults read at least one magazine regularly, 50% of American adults attend at least one movie a month, and 30% of the American adult population read books (Emery, Ault and Agee, 1965:131).

The various mass media vigorously compete with each other for the consumer's attention and advertising dollars. Yet, as Head observes, the media "Interrelate in complex ways which turn out in the long run to be mutually helpful. They use each other's material and talent; they invest in each other's stock; they benefit from each other's technological developments" (Head, 1972:315).

Thus, for example, *TV Guide* is a magazine devoted to the television industry, ABC's parent company owns motion picture theaters, Hollywood makes movie films for TV, TV makes films for Hollywood, and media firms own both broadcast stations and newspapers.

In comparing the various media, one may find the electronic media superior to the print media in some characteristics, inferior in others. Thus, several studies have shown that the more educated people are, the more they tend to favor print over the electronic media (Schramm, 1973:182).

But other studies have shown that television is most believable, would be most desired if people were limited to one medium, and is rated as giving the best performance of all the media—and that TV increased its leadership in these dimensions from 1959 to 1967 (Roper, 1967:1, 3, 11).

The various types of mass media may be compared on other dimensions, too. These include:

1. The medium's fidelity in presenting the following dimensions of an original event: (a) verbal symbols, (b) picture symbols, (c) color, (d) sound, and (e) motion (Merrill and Lowenstein, 1971:19).

2. The medium's delivery speed—the length of time between an event and when the medium is able to inform people about it.

3. The medium's portability—the ease with which the medium can be moved about the environment both to (a) represent or "cover" an event and (b) to reach people with its message.

4. The reviewability of the message as presented by the medium—the ease with which a message receiver can have the message repeated to satisfy his needs.

5. The extensiveness of the medium's coverage of the environment—how much information of potential interest the medium can make available to message receivers.

6. The medium's accessibility to feedback—the ease with which a message receiver can feed back to the medium his reaction to the medium's message.

From another perspective, the mass media may be thought of as the complex of human organizations that directly produce communications devices, such as newspapers and magazines as organizations, radio and TV stations and networks, book publishing firms, publishers of circulars, and so on.

Closely related to mass media organizations are several other important human institutions. These "adjuncts" to the mass media depend on the media organizations, but the media organizations, in turn, depend on them. (Emery, Ault and Agee, 1965:9.) They are:

1. Press associations, which collect and distribute news and pictures to newspapers, television and radio networks and individual stations, and news magazines.

2. Syndicates, which provide background news and pictures, commentary, and entertainment features to newspapers, magazines, television and radio stations and networks.

3. Advertising agencies, which produce and distribute advertising materials for publication or broadcast, thus, serving both business clients and the media organizations.

4. Advertising and public relations departments of business institutions which serve merchandising and information roles for their firms.

5. Public relations counseling and publicity firms, which advise clients and offer to media organizations information on behalf of clients.

6. Research organizations, which study the impact of mass media messages and other aspects of mass communications.

Press. Today the term press is usually meant to include the four major media of mass communication—newspapers, magazines, radio and television, as well as other adjuncts such as press associations that gather and disseminate information for public consumption.

The definition, however, has shifted with the times. At the turn of the century, the term press—from whence came the name—was confined to the media produced by printing presses, that is, newspapers and a few journals. Later, during the decades of the 1930's and 1940's, for instance, it also included radio and cinema news—a very popular and common part of the film industry. In the 1950's, cinema news dropped out, displaced by the new giant, television.

The press can also be approached from the point of view of coverage. Thus, one finds media representing international press, national press, regional press, and local press, in addition to such categories as trade press, sports press, and others.

Beyond this, the term is no longer reserved for reporters only. It now includes new analysts, commentators, editors, photojournalists, and technical writers as well as reporters.

18 | TELECOMMUNICATION

A PRODUCT OF the industrial revolution, telecommunication is the process of communicating over a distance using electromagnetic instruments designed for that purpose.

Some sub-divisions of telecommunication include:

Mass telecommunication. That aspect of mass communication which limits itself to transmission via telecommunication instruments. Mass telecommunication includes commercial radio and television, educational television, cable television, and other such activities.

Point-to-point telecommunication. A special type of communication that uses electromagnetic instruments to cover distance—as does mass communication—but shares audience characteristics with interpersonal, or face-to-face, communication. Point-to-point telecommunication includes the telephone, teletype, telegraph, mobile radio, air-to-ground radio, ship-to-shore radio, and other similar telecommunication systems.

Surveillance telecommunication. A special type of communication that uses electromagnetic instruments for the purpose of "scanning the horizon" for danger signals. Surveillance telecommunication include radar, atmospheric pollution monitoring, weather satellite, and other such telecommunication systems.

The part played in the communication systems of a mass society by telecommunication cannot be overemphasized. Indeed, telecommunication is considered by most to be the heart of the society-wide communication networks.

8 | Informal Channels of Communication. 9 | Formal Channels of Communication. 15 | Medio Communication. 16 | Mass Communication.

19 | NON-VERBAL COMMUNICATION

WHILE MOST of the interaction that takes place in our society is carried by spoken and visual symbols, much meaningful communication is also non-verbal. Non-verbal communication is the transfer of meaning involving the absence of symbolic sound or sound representations.

Popularly, it is called the "silent language."

Following Duncan (1969), non-verbal communication can be classified as follows:

1. Body motion or kinesic behavior. This category includes gestures and other body movements, including facial expression, eye movement, and posture.

2. Paralanguage. This category includes voice qualities, speech non-fluencies, laughing, yawning, and grunting.

3. Proxemics. This category includes human use and perception of the physical space.

4. Olfaction.

5. Skin sensitivity to touch and temperature.

6. Use of artifacts. This category includes such things as dress and cosmetics.

Although the scientific study of non-verbal communication is in its infancy, the first three categories have drawn considerable research attention as of late and the body of knowledge has expanded significantly. With each, an important pioneering researcher has been associated with it—Ray Birdwhistell with kinesics, George Trager with paralanguage, and Edward T. Hall with proxemics (Lin, 1973:68).

Non-verbal communication is culture-bound. That is to say, it is not instinctive human nature. Rather, non-verbal communication is learned behavior, acquired through the process of informal socialization. Consequently, it is markedly different behavior from culture to culture.

1 | Communication.   3 | Symbol.   5 | Message.

20 | POLITICAL COMMUNICATION

POLITICAL COMMUNICATION is communication that has actual or potential effects on the functioning of a political state or other political entity.

Political communication is a pervasive activity. As Almond and Coleman note:

> All of the functions performed in the political system—political socialization and recruitment, interest articulation, interest aggregation, rule-making, rule application, and rule adjudication—are performed *by means* of communication. Parents, teachers, and priests, for example, impart political socialization through communication. Interest group leaders and representatives and party leaders perform their articulation and aggregation functions by communicating demands and policy recommendations. Legislators enact laws on the basis of information communicated to them and by communicating with one another and with other elements of the political system. In performing their functions, bureaucrats receive and analyze information from the society and from various parts of the polity. Similarly, the judicial process is carried on by means of communication. (Almond and Coleman, 1960:4–5.)

Traditionally, those in power have controlled communication to achieve their goals; for example, to stay in power. Thus, whether despots or democrats, political leaders tend to manipulate the information available to citizens.

> The great historical empires, as well as modern large states have been characterized by the appearance of specialized communication structures and by the expenditure of important resources to facilitate communication flows. The Mongol hordes of Genghis Khan, for example, were linked by an elaborate system of mail riders (much like the American Pony Express) which could cross the steppes of Asia with remarkable speed. From the drummers, runners, and smoke signals of primitive tribes, through medi-

17 | Mass Media.   25 | Public Relations.   26 | Propaganda.
31 | Communicator's Intent.   32 | Mass Communication Activities.

eval heralds, to the presidential press conference and bureaucratic "memo," political systems have created special communication structures to accomplish their purpose. (Almond and Powell, 1966.)

No less than those who rule, those seeking to rule, or trying to get the political system to take certain desired actions, or to change the system itself also exploit or try to exploit the communications process to their own advantage—such as in releasing selected information to the press or staging public demonstrations to call attention to a cause or an issue. For example, two teach-ins held in Utrecht, The Netherlands, in 1967, sought to rouse public opinion against a city urban renewal plan. Bothe and van Koutrik concluded that the teach-ins were indeed political events, that they mobilized persons of varied opinions and attracted press attention (Bothe and van Koutrik, 1968:258–272).

Power, of course, is a central concept in political science. The political system defines how power and influence shall be allocated and exercised, whether as in a dictatorship or a representative democracy. But communication is crucial in the exercise of power. Thus, as Fagen observes:

> We cannot conceive of the exercise of power by individual A over individual B without some communication from A to B. This communicatory activity may be as direct and open as caveman A's threat to bash caveman B unless the latter hands over his catch. Or, the activity may be as indirect and difficult to isolate as the web of messages, perceptions, and expectations which ultimately enables the Prime Minister to convince the leader of the opposition to support him on a crucial issue. But in both cases, when individuals are in a relationship of power or influence, they are also of necessity in communication. (Fagen, 1966:5.)

Several important institutions are used for political communication:

1. *Organizations:* parties, unions, public bureaucracies, and other mass organizations capable of linking the elite, sub-elite, and broad sectors of the citizenry. These are relatively national in scope, relatively permanent.

2. *Groups:* less permanent, less institutionalized and often less pervasive collectivities, such as "Housewives for Johnson."

3. *Mass Media:* both in enabling the elites to talk with one another and in linking the elites to other chains such as interpersonal networks, organizations, etc.

4. *Specialized Channels:* demonstrations and special events used for the aggregation and articulation of interests under special circumstances. (Fagen, 1966:37–49.)

International political communication is used by national states to influence the behavior of people in other national states. This includes propaganda and information of most government agencies. Such communication is usually, although not always, an auxiliary instrument of policy, used along with diplomatic, economic, or military measures (Davison and George, 1970:461, 463).

International political communication has become an important fact of life.

> Even a casual observer of the media of mass communication cannot fail to notice that men's minds—nationally and internationally—are being subjected to a ceaseless and clever bombardment of messages. These messages are calculated to influence and control. Internationally, these propagandistic messages are either directed against real or potential enemies, or at "neutral" message consumers who might be won over. In addition, of course, much of the international media effort is aimed at reinforcing "friendly" images held in other nations of the country engaged in the propaganda effort. (Fischer and Merrill, 1970:175.)

But this is not to suggest that a national political leader or administration can so control communication so as to do as pleased. They can and do influence communication—but so do many others, with different goals. Thus, a political leader must take this into account as he charts his own course of action. As Gordon and Falk note:

> Technology alone, naturally, means nothing. What men do with it is everything. And what they will do with modern mass communications technology is to lay bare for all mankind to hear (or at least receive impressions of) the manifold ways in which the world's cultures are, at any time, interacting one with the other. Neither international agreements, the protocol of diplomacy, nor "Top Secret" stamps in the hands of generals will vitiate communication technology's power, when all is said and done to *create conditions with which foreign policies of every nation must eventually recognize a priori*. Nothing, as the French Sociologist Jacques Ellul has trenchantly shown, can muster enough power to stop them except weapons of total lethal destruction. (Gordon and Falk, 1973:313–314.)

Part Three

WHAT IS COMMUNICATED

21 | NEWS

A SIMPLE DEFINITION of news is that of Turner Catledge of the New York *Times:* "News is anything you didn't know yesterday."

As this definition indicates, news involves *new information.* The first moon landing was news when it happened July 20, 1969; it was not news in 1970.

News is not an event or happening; rather it is the report of such (Charnley, 1966:23). A murder is not news until it is discovered and reported.

News is the report of something new that *interests a particular audience,* whether worldwide, nationwide, or one limited by geographical, cultural, economic, or other interests. A report on a new hybrid corn variety is more important news in rural Iowa than in industrial Massachusetts.

The "news worthiness" of an event is affected by several factors. These include (a) where it happened in reference to audience members, (b) the extent to which that event personally affects audience members, (c) the prominence of those involved in the event, (d) the competition of other news events at that moment.

News is *information people urgently need* in getting their bearings in a rapidly changing world. Where the situation is ambiguous, or there are alternatives, or a decision has to be made, any new information that might affect the outcome is news. News is information that is important to someone. News is *perishable.* Once an event or situation is understood and the tension it has aroused eases, the accepted information becomes history. It is still interesting, but it no longer is pressing, no longer news (Shibutani, 1966:39–41).

5 | Message. 14 | Rumor. 22 | Editorial/Editorializing. 23 | Objective Journalism. 26 | Propaganda. 32 | Mass Communication Activities.

NEWS VALUES

Any newsworthy disruption or potential disruption of the status quo, writes Harriss and Johnson, will be due to events and potentials which are characterized by one or more of the following news values:

Intrinsic Characteristics of the Event

1. Conflict (tension—surprise)
2. Progress (triumph—achievement)
3. Disaster (defeat—destruction)
4. Consequence (effect upon community)
5. Eminence (prominence)
6. Novelty (the unusual and even the extremely usual)
7. Human interest (emotional background)

Desirable Qualifications

8. Timeliness (freshness and newness)
9. Proximity (local appeal)

General Interest

10. Sex
11. Animals

From Julian Harriss and Stanley Johnson, *The Complete Reporter,* New York: The Macmillan Company, 1965, pp. 32–33.

22 | EDITORIAL / EDITORIALIZING

AN EDITORIAL is a published article or a broadcast arguing the opinion of the owner or management of a media outlet, usually on a matter of public concern. To editorialize is to express an editorial opinion about something.

Newspapers have devoted a special column or an entire page or two to editorials for more than a century. However, they did not consciously separate editorial comment from news until early in the 20th century, when objective news reporting was generally adopted.

At first, the Federal Communications Commission prohibited broadcasters from presenting their opinions on the air, arguing that the air waves were a limited public resource. However, in 1949, the Commission reversed itself and encouraged the broadcast media to editorialize.

Radio and television stations, and to some extent magazines, have adopted the newspaper practice of physically separating news from editorial comment.

The newspaper editorial page serves the reader in at least five ways, as identified by Waldrop:

1. To bring order to the chaos of the glut of occurrences, save him from becoming "news-drunk," provide a "pattern of meaning in the confusion and complexity of events";

2. Fight his battles, defending his liberties, protecting him from government, and as Mr. Dooley said, comforting the afflicted and afflicting the comfortable;

3. Set him to thinking, free him from myths, shatter illusions, provide a forum wherein the dialogue that is necessary for democracy is held;

4. Plough and cultivate public opinion so that when decisions are to be made, the climate of opinion will depend not on emotions of the moment but on long-continued education and debate;

5. Enable him to be on guard against the editor's human weakness in presenting and playing the news. (Waldrop, 1967:4.)

The editorial page serves the newspaper, too. It is:

1. A source of personality, of "conscience, courage and convictions";

2. A means of demonstrating that "A newspaper is a citizen of its community," a statement which appears in the editorial masthead of the Eugene *Register-Guard;*

3. "A leaven and a guide" to the whole newspaper operation. (Waldrop, 1967:5.)

Traditionally, newspaper editorials have been published on an anonymous basis, with the implication that the editorial speaks for the newspaper, not the writer as an individual. The editorial "we" rather than the personal "I" is used, or the first person pronoun is avoided altogether. However, as editorial writers acknowledge, the personal views and interests of the editorial writers are strongly represented in these writings. At the editorial board meetings at which editorial topics are discussed and perhaps agreement reached on the stance to be taken in particular editorials, the customary practice is to let the writer who agrees with the position to be taken and is informed and deeply interested in the subject actually do the editorial in question (Hulteng, 1973:27).

In recent years a few newspapers have adopted a pro-con editorial policy, presenting in the same issue matching columns arguing two sides of a controversial issue.

Broadcast editorials are less anonymous than newspaper editorials. Radio listeners may hear a voice they recognize, and TV viewers see a familiar station representative, perhaps a broadcast executive, delivering the station editorial. But even then, the fact that the editorial represents the broadcast outlet's corporate position is emphasized, and use of the first person singular is avoided.

Some newspapers are criticized for "Afghanistanism," a practice of editorializing on non-local issues unlikely to disturb readers or listeners while neglecting to say anything about what is happening in city hall or elsewhere in the local community where the media operates.

23 | OBJECTIVE JOURNALISM

OBJECTIVE JOURNALISM—the presentation of news in a factual, unbiased, largely impersonal way—became the ideal of American journalism about the turn of the century.

With the invention of the telegraph, news wire services began transmitting their news to newspapers with widely differing viewpoints. Thus the Associated Press and the United Press (later to become United Press International) found it necessary to write their reports as factually as possible, to omit the writer's own opinions. The idea of objectivity was adopted by newspapers, and later by radio and TV stations and broadcast networks.

The objective-type journalism replaced the personal journalism of the 19th century, which had been characterized by opinionated partisan "news" in newspapers often founded to promote particular viewpoints.

Objective journalism means presenting the facts of an event as it actually happens, of a situation as it actually exists. It is an accurate, balanced, fair presentation of the facts, one untainted by personal bias or outside influence.

> Journalistic objectivity is a state of mind on the reporter's and editor's part that includes a conscious effort not to prejudge what he sees, not to be influenced by his own personal preconceptions, predilections, allegiances and biases; not to be swayed by the rhetoric of participants; always to assume there is "another side" and to make an effort to see to it that the other side has a chance to be heard. (Westley, 1972:75.)

The keynote of this school of thought is that journalists should strive for objectivity lest the press lose the confidence of its audience in today's pluralistic society.

Objective journalism often is faulted in not giving readers a perspective of events. Charnley puts it this way:

21 | News.   22 | Editorial/Editorializing.   25 | Public Relations.
26 | Propaganda.   44 | Freedom of the Press.   46 | Gatekeeper.

Objective reporting assumes that the consumer, with his own resources, with no hints from the news story, is able to apply appropriate perspective to whatever facts the story gives him: to separate the genuine from the phony, the pure from the adulterated, the true from the false, the fair from the biased, the complete from the incomplete, the trustworthy and benevolent from the dishonorable and malicious. Even in the nineteenth century it was a rare thing that a news consumer could accomplish such an overwhelming feat; today it is more rare. The modern world is so complex that no man can grasp it all, let alone evaluate its parts. No matter how much news he is given, the everyday citizen cannot untangle the mass of facts and forces and frustrations without some form of background or interpretation to guide him. In truth, the very mass of news so overwhelms him that he often gives up hope and escapes to the comics, the movies or the latest television series about physicians. (Charnely, 1966:25.)

Objective journalism may be considered the polar opposite of advocacy journalism, which is viewed both as a recent innovation and as the 20th century reincarnation of the old personal journalism of the 19th century. Advocacy journalism developed as certain writers, disenchanted by establishment notions of balanced news, objectivity and reliance on traditional news sources, sought and were granted opportunity to advocate their own viewpoints in "news" articles in conventional papers. Advocacy journalism "screams for a particular cause and tends to be dogmatic and uncompromising" (Izard, Culbertson and Lambert, 1973:214).

Related to advocacy journalism is another new development, "The New Journalism," a subjective, creative, and candid style of reportage and commentary (Johnson, 1971:xi). New journalism seeks to present a true picture of an event or situation through the techniques of the fiction writer. These include intimate description and detail, dramatic presentation, fictious but life-like dialogue, and sometimes first person participation in the event. The writer makes no pretense of being objective. His writing is a very subjective, personal presentation in which he reveals his personality and commitment, how he feels about the events he encountered, a "tell-it-like-I-feel-it" kind of journalism.

Critics object that New Journalists play loose with facts, take liberties in commenting on them, and shuffle events around for dramatic or political effect. They compare the New Journalist with an underground editor who refuses to allow facts to stand in the way of presenting a political or doctrinaire point of view. Proponents say the New Journalism permits the reader better to experience and enjoy the total situation because in such experience lies real truth. They say such truth can be found in the intentions and emotional tone of people's behavior and not in the factual situation (Izard, Culbertson and Lambert, 1973:212–13).

Truman Capote, Norman Mailer, Tom Wolfe, Gay Talese, and Jimmy Breslin are examples of the New Journalists. Some of these wrote conventional news stories for metropolitan newspapers before turning to the New Journalism. The term New Journalism also is applied to writers of the underground press, who see themselves not only as reporting but making a revolution (Johnson, 1971:3).

Investigative reporting, interpretive reporting, and depth reporting are other terms that figure in discussions of objective journalism. These are sometimes used rather interchangeably to suggest thorough but objective reporting and writing, as in this definition of depth reporting by T. C. Harris, executive editor of the *St. Petersburg Times:*

"We regard depth reporting as telling the reader all the essential facts about the subject, the whys and the wherefores of it, as many sides of it as we can get, and plenty of background" (Copple, 1964:19).

In a more limited sense, the term investigative reporting may be used to describe the probing and reporting on corruption in government, business and elsewhere, often on a team basis. Thus used, it may be likened to the muckraking journalism of earlier decades.

Frequently, interpretive reporting is used to suggest putting news in its proper perspective, giving factual background, recalling for example what the governor said last year on the issue under consideration as well as what he said about it today. In this sense, interpretive journalism means explaining, amplifying and clarifying situations for readers (MacDougall, 1968:17).

Still other terms that are germane to a discussion of journalistic objectivity are involvement, activism, and credibility. In this context, involvement refers to the dependency relationship a newsman presumably assumes when he accepts favors from a news source. For example, a newsman accepting gifts or "freebies" such as free airplane junkets to Europe paid for by organizations or individuals seeking favorable news treatment. It also may include pressures to seek favorable news treatment which a news executive encounters when he becomes an officer in an organization that desires improved press coverage.

Activism refers to the aggressive behavior of journalists who participate in protest marches, wear armbands and badges, sign petitions and in other ways publicly demonstrate their views on controversial issues in the news.

Credibility has to do with whether or not a newsman's performance warrants esteem, praise, or belief from disinterested (as opposed to uninterested) parties; it is a dimension of trustworthiness with which a public views a mass medium (or, in some instances, the press as a whole). Observers note that both activism and involvement tend to negatively affect the credibility of the press.

24 | ADVERTISING / PUBLICITY

ADVERTISING IS THE presentation and promotion of a product, service or idea where such presentation and promotion is identified with and paid for by a sponsor.

Publicity, by contrast, is the presentation of news or editorial comment about a product, service or idea where such presentation is not identified with and paid for by a sponsor.

Both advertising and publicity are nonpersonal—they both use the mass media rather than personal contact. But there are important differences between the two concepts. Advertising seeks not only to inform, but to promote—for example, to persuade people to buy a product or service. Publicity seeks to inform, though by informing it may have the side effect of promoting a product or service.

A publicity news item may fall into one of three classes: it may be presented to the public as researched and written in a publicity "release" prepared by the sponsor; it may be presented as researched and written by the media organization; or it may be presented as something between these two extremes. From the standpoint of the sponsor, publicity may be classed as favorable, unfavorable, or something in-between, depending on the image presented.

Advertising messages are prepared by writers, artists, and other skilled craftsmen working for the concern sponsoring the advertisement and for advertising agencies who represent the sponsors. These messages are disseminated to the public as display and classified advertisements in newspapers and magazines and as "commercials" on radio and TV.

Advertising may be classified as (1) commercial advertising, including (a) consumer and (b) business advertising, and (2) noncommercial advertising, such as that by governments, charitable institutions, political groups and the like.

Consumer advertising is addressed to those who use a product or a service to satisfy a personal or household need.

Business advertising may include:

1. Industrial advertising—addressed primarily to management people in an industrial plant.
2. Professional advertising—addressed to those practicing recognized professions like law and medicine.
3. Vocational and management advertising—addressed to persons in specialized vocations.
4. Trade advertising—addressed to merchants reselling products for a profit.

From the standpoint of what it seeks to accomplish, advertising may be classified as:

1. *Product reputation advertising*—designed to sell goods or services.

2. *Institutional advertising*—designed to achieve other objectives, such as the selling of an idea. It has three forms:

   a. Patronage institutional advertising—to sell the idea of patronizing a producer or retailer for reasons other than specific product merits.
   b. Public relations institutional advertising—designed to improve the firm's image or reputation.
   c. Public service institutional advertising—to promote noncontroversial causes in the interest of the public.

Advertising may be classified in terms of the type of appeal it makes:

1. Direct action or "hard sell"—aggressively urging action.
2. Indirect action or "soft sell"—subtly suggesting action.

Advertising may also be classified in terms of the media used to transmit the message: newspaper advertising, radio advertising, television advertising, and so on.

Advertising may be classified on a geographical basis:

1. *National advertising* promotes a product or service in all major markets. It employs the national media, such as network TV or radio and national magazines as well as regional and local media.
2. *Regional advertising* is addressed to a well-defined geographical area with common economic interests, such as a wholesale trade area, for example, a three-state area served by a

banking chain. Regional advertising may employ national as well as regional and local media. Thus, a bank may choose to run its advertising message only in those copies of *Time* magazine that reach readers in the bank's business region. (This is made possible by the magazine's practice of splitting its press run, publishing different advertisements on a given page depending on the geographical area to which the magazine is to be sent.)

3. *Local advertising* refers to advertising by a retail firm done in media which mainly reach persons residing in the city where the retail firm is located. An example, a newspaper ad for a local food store or restaurant.

Publicity has some advantages over advertising. It costs the sponsor nothing. It is accepted more readily by those to whom it is directed. Thus sponsors work hard to get favorable publicity for the product, service or idea they are promoting. This has led to the "pseudo-event"—a happening staged to secure news coverage. A "press conference" called when there was no real news and a ribbon-cutting ceremony are examples of events manufactured to manipulate rather than to inform (Safire, 1968:362).

25 | PUBLIC RELATIONS

PUBLIC RELATIONS, as it is most generally understood, is a planned program of action to gain favorable public opinion for an organization or individual.

As expressed by Christian, public relations is a "conscious effort to motivate or influence people through communication to think well of an organization, to respect it, to support it, and to stick with it through trial and trouble" (Cutlip and Center, 1958:6).

The term public relations sometimes is employed to characterize the quality of an institution's relationship to its various publics, as indicated by the expression, "The government has bad public relations."

However, herein the term is used to describe means to attain desired relationships with the public, not the quality of the relationships themselves.

Viewed from this perspective, public relations has three main and historic functions: informing people, persuading people, and integrating people with people (Bernays, 1952:12).

This third element, integrating people with people, is sometimes overlooked as the concept of public relations is examined. But as Bernays observes, public relations is a vital tool of adjustment, interpretation, and integration between individuals, groups, and society. Public understanding is basic to existence in our competitive system. To know how to get along with the public is important for everyone . . . through public relations, an individual or group can ensure that public decisions are based on knowledge and understanding (Bernays, 1952:7, 8).

An outgrowth of the complexity of modern society, public relations is a management function of nearly every organization today—whether a business firm, a government agency, a labor union, a university, or some other agency. The objective is to gain the sup-

22 | Editorial/Editorializing.   24 | Advertising/Publicity.   26 | Propaganda.   28 | Attitude/Opinion.   32 | Mass Communication Activities.   42 | Public Opinion.   48 | Mass Society/Mass Culture.

port and cooperation of people whom the organization desires to affect.

> Public relations started as publicity—now just one of its phases—because, as it became harder for people with different backgrounds to understand and know about each other, the first necessity was for one group to tell others about itself. In developing, public relations has come to include a great many other functions besides telling about someone or some group. It also tells the group what others think of it; it helps the group determine what it must do to get the good will of others; it plans ways and means of winning that good will; and it carries on activities designed to win it. In the process of doing these things, it encompasses a great many functions, concepts, and techniques. (Lesly, 1950:4–5).

A rather rigorous, explicit definition of public relations is an oft-quoted one by *Public Relations News:*

"Public relations is the management function which evaluates public attitudes, identifies the policies and procedures of an individual or an organization with the public interest, and executes a program of action to earn public understanding and acceptance."

This definition suggests that public relations practitioners have a threefold function:

> 1. To ascertain and evaluate public opinion.
> 2. To counsel management in ways of dealing with public opinion as it exists.
> 3. To use communication to influence public opinion.

Such terms as press agentry, product promotion, publicity, institutional advertising, and lobbying all have been associated with public relations. But they are not synonymous with public relations. Rather, they are tools of public relations, though tools like press agentry now are in disrepute after having given public relations itself a bad image.

The public relation practitioner is a communications specialist hired to do the following:

> 1. To facilitate and insure an inflow of representative opinions from an organization's several publics in order that its policies and operations may be kept compatible with the diverse needs and views of these publics.
> 2. To counsel management on ways and means of shaping its policies and operations to gain maximum public acceptance for what it deems essential in the best interests of all concerned.
> 3. To interpret widely and favorably an organization's policies and operations. (Cutlip and Center, 1958:6.)

An organization may take care of its public relations needs by one or a combination of these methods:

1. It may set up its own public relations staff, including a full-time staff official and several assistants.

2. It may buy the services of an independent public relations counselor, who may also represent other clients with non-conflicting interests.

3. It may use the public relations services of an advertising agency, perhaps the same agency that handles the organization's advertising. (Cutlip and Center, 1958:7.)

Most public relations practitioners point to the turn of the century as the definite beginning of their profession. Yet the public relations function was not too widespread among American organizations until the post-World War II era. It was then that the term "public relations" became a household word.

As an academic discipline, training for public relations work is usually housed in schools of journalism or related programs, since the tools of communication are the basic tools of the practitioner.

26 | PROPAGANDA

PROPAGANDA IS expresssion of opinion or action by individuals or groups deliberately designed to influence opinions or actions of other individuals or groups to predetermined ends (Institute for Propaganda Analysis, 1937).

A characteristic of propaganda is that an attempt is often made to have a view accepted not on its own merits but by appealing to other motives—for example, by playing upon emotional attitudes and feelings. Another characteristic is that propaganda is often a one-sided—as opposed to a two-sided—effort to gain acceptance of a particular view.

As a mass-communicated activity, propaganda tends to have short-run, situationally-defined aims. The appeal is to

> . . . a diverse population on the basis of immediate interest, fears, or desires. The propaganda of advertisers, interest groups, and political parties is largely of this kind. The objective is not so much to influence the individual deeply as to win his support for some immediate issue, candidate, or product. The more short-run and superficial the aims, the easier it is to use propaganda tricks and gadgets. Long-run aims, which attempt to change basic attitudes, are more difficult to achieve.
>
> Although it seems obvious that the objective of propaganda is to win active approval, in fact it may seek only passive acquiescence. (Broom and Selznick, 1963:282.)

Behavioral scientists have further classified propaganda into white propaganda and black propaganda. White propaganda is that type of propaganda which the propagandized perceive as coming from a source outside their own ranks. Black propaganda is that propaganda which is perceived as coming from within their own ranks.

Seven propaganda devices have been identified. They include: *Name calling device:* giving an idea a bad label. It is used to

20 | Political Communication. 28 | Attitude/Opinion. 32 | Mass Communication Activities. 42 | Public Opinion. 43 | Public Opinion Process.

make us reject and condemn an idea or program without examining the evidence.

Glittering generality device: associating something with a "virtue word." It is used to make us accept and approve something without examining the evidence.

Transfer device: carrying the authority, sanction, and prestige of something respected and revered over to something else in order to make the latter acceptable. It also carries authority, sanction, and disapproval to cause us to reject and disapprove something the propagandist would have us reject and disapprove.

Testimonial device: having some respected or hated person say that a given idea or program or person is good or bad.

Plain folks device: the method by which a speaker attempts to convince his audience that he and his ideas are good because they are "of the people"—the "plain folks."

Card stacking device: involves the selection and use of facts or falsehoods, illustrations or distractions, and logical or illogical statements, in order to give the best or the worst possible case for an idea, program, person, or product.

Band wagon device: here the theme is "Everybody—at least all of us—is doing it." Consequently, the propagandist attempts to convince us that all members of a group to which we belong are accepting his program and that we must therefore follow our crowd and "jump on the band wagon."

Part Four

PROCESS AND EFFECTS

27 | SOCIALIZATION

SOCIALIZATION IS A life-long socio-psychological process in which the individual makes as a part of himself the norms, values, and behavior patterns which his society emphasizes.

The infant child does not enter this world with the ability to participate in group activity; rather, the child is born a biological organism—with the capacity to learn. Through imitation, trial and error, rote exercises, and many other processes he learns to respond to the symbols about him in a manner appropriate in his society.

This capacity to communicate symbolically makes it possible for man to acquire—and, as importantly, to pass on—a cultural heritage. Apart from socialization, this could not be realized.

Socialization, as Wilson notes, is the process of entering the human group—or being inducted—into the secrets of society:

> It is a process in which a number of minor miracles occur: the animal becomes a human being, sheer behavior is transformed into conduct, the individual as an organic unit becomes a person, self-aware and able to guide his conduct in terms of the increasingly subtle cues that signal others' expectation. (Wilson, 1966:90.)

Finally, the socialization process is often dichotomized into formal and informal. What one learns from his friends, family, and others in informal settings is known as *informal socialization*. In contrast, when the situation is structured, the learning process is said to be *formal socialization*. The school is an example of this type of socialization.

In modern society, the mass media is increasingly an important agent in both informal and formal socialization. Television, motion pictures, and magazines, particularly, have become important sources of socialization for children and young adults, replacing much of the influence enjoyed by the family (parents) in earlier periods. For all, in a world that is constantly in a state of change, the

2 | Language. 3 | Symbol. 30 | Selective Exposure/Perception/Retention. 32 | Mass Communication Activities.

mass media stand as an authoritative voice where other agencies do not. Finally, the factor of time—that is, the large amount of time—which people spend with the media place them in the forefront of socializing agents.

28 | ATTITUDE / OPINION

PERHAPS THE SINGLE most important concept in the lexicon of the social psychologist, if not all behavioral scientists, is that of attitude. Despite its widespread use, however, the concept is a difficult one to operationalize, and many different definitions of an attitude are used.

Berkowitz (1972:47) identifies three major schools of thought concerning the concept. Adherents of one school think of an attitude as an evaluation or feeling reaction. An individual's attitude toward a social object is viewed as a feeling of favorableness or unfavorableness. Another school conceives of an attitude as a readiness to respond in a particular way regarding some social object. This readiness is conceptualized as pro or con in nature. A third school sees an attitude as an interlocking set of understandings, feelings, and actions toward a social object.

This last viewpoint—involving the cognitive, affective, and conative components—is emerging as, perhaps, the most widely accepted school of thought.

An attitude, then, according to this school of thought, is a continuing set of interlocking components—including beliefs and evaluations (the cognitive component), feelings and emotions (the affective component), and the behavioral readiness (the action component)—concerning some social object.

While not stated, the three components are identifiable in other popular definitions of an attitude. For example, Goode's (1959:1) definition reflects many definitions currently in use: An attitude is the tendency to act or react positively or negatively to something, based on the individual's values, and rooted in his social experience. Here one sees the three components noted above.

Opinion. An opinion is the product of an individual's attitudes. Given certain conditions in his social environment, the individual arranges his attitudes into hierarchies. When the individual speaks or writes he is expressing his attitudinal hierarchy—he is giving an opinion. When shifts take place in the external situation, shifts take

26 | Propaganda. 29 | Attitude Change. 42 | Public Opinion.
57 | Polls. 58 | Content Analysis.

place in the hierarchy of attitudes as well, and new arrangements are called forth—leading to new opinions. An opinion, then, is an expression of an attitude in words.

While attitudes and opinions are less ambiguous than in previous years, in their popular work, *Human Behavior,* Berelson and Steiner still felt the necessity to label this topic OAB's (o-abs), or opinion, attitude, and beliefs (1964:557), with the notation that they do not have fixed meanings.

This lack of a fixed meaning has led to some confusion. Gordon and Falk (1973:84) report that pollsters often take advantage of this situation and frequently evaluate any number of factors except attitudes in so-called attitude studies.

29 | ATTITUDE CHANGE

THE STUDY OF attitude change is the attempt to identify and understand the processes underlying the modification of attitudes (Wagner and Sherwood, 1969).

Messages from any type of communication—interpersonal, medio, or mass—are capable of initiating any one of several types of attitude modification. These include:

Attitude reinforcement. Sometimes called congruent attitude change, reinforcement is a strengthening of the existing attitude. An attitude is a positive or negative evaluation; hence, it can be given a positive (+) or negative (−) sign. Thus, attitude reinforcement can be called an attitude shift in the direction of the existing sign.

Attitude change. Sometimes called incongruent attitude change, to change an attitude is to effect a shift so that the attitude now takes on the opposite sign, for instance, from positive to negative. Equivalent to conversion.

Boomerang effect. A shift in the attitude in the direction opposite to that intended.

Conservation. The maintenance of existing attitudes; messages designed to prevent an attitude from shifting.

Neutralization. The shifting of an attitude to the neutral zone; in other words, the attitude does not have any strong pro or con action tendencies.

Ceiling effect. The reinforcing of an attitude to the extent that any additional reinforcement cannot be measured.

TYPES OF ATTITUDE CHANGE

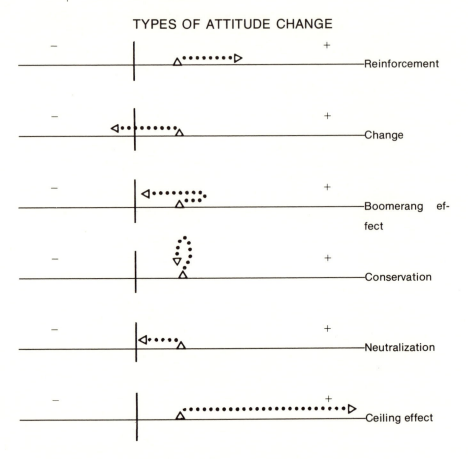

Note: Arrows indicate the shift that has taken place.

30 | SELECTIVE EXPOSURE /
PERCEPTION / RETENTION

THE THREE HIGHLY interrelated concepts of selective exposure, selective perception, and selective retention do much to shed light on the behavior of social man. Although there are three separate phenomena involved, because of their close interrelationship, some behavioral scientists group all three concepts together under the one term, selective perception.

Selective Exposure. This is the tendency for people to expose themselves to communications in accordance with their existing opinions and interests and to avoid communications not in accordance with their existing opinions and interests (Klapper, 1960). Although self-selection of exposure in line with predispositions is mainly conscious and deliberate, according to Berelson and Steiner (1964), selective exposure can also operate non-consciously as well.

Selective perception. This is the tendency for people to misperceive and misinterpret persuasive communications in accordance with their own predispositions, by distorting the message in a direction favorable to those predispositions (Berelson and Steiner, 1964). Thus, one person can "hear" the speaker saying one thing while another person can "hear" the same speaker saying something different. Theoretically, there could be "heard" as many different versions of the same message as there are listeners.

Selective Retention. Selective perception may obviously involve selective retention as well, notes Klapper (1960). The line of demarcation between the two processes is, in fact, often difficult and, in some instances, impossible to draw; but in brief, material is more readily learned by the sympathetic and more readily forgotten by the unsympathetic.

Even in extreme cases, say Berelson and Steiner (1964:531), self-selection of communication exposure in line with predispositions is far from complete. Consequently, there is usually a sizeable minority

3 | Symbol. 6 | Communication Noise. 27 | Socialization. 28 | Attitude/Opinion. 29 | Attitude Change.

of people who, out of curiosity, or accident, etc., read and listen to material against or indifferent to their own position. But most importantly people tend to see or hear communications to the degree to which they are readily available.

31 | THE COMMUNICATOR'S INTENT

COMMUNICATORS HAVE varying intentions, whether they transmit their messages through the informal channel of face-to-face conversation or through the formal channels of a newspaper or magazine. In fact, says Gordon (1971:37), intension is probably a quality of all communications, just as "motivation" (as the word is usually used by psychologists) is involved with all behavior—as long as the communication and/or behavior involves human beings.

A communicator may not even intend to affect others. Thus his expression may be *egocentric*, completely expressive in nature and independent of any listener. Small children may chatter incessantly, taking little note of potential listeners. Adults may write poetry solely for themselves.

However, a communicator usually speaks or writes to others, and in doing so takes cognizance of others' views. In this, the communicator's expression is *socialized* expression, and its intention is to communicate, to affect others.

A communicator's intent may also be *manifest* or *latent*. A manifest intent is one that is recognized and intended. If a communicator disseminates a message to increase the listener's understanding about the communicator's position on a public issue, his action could be classified as a manifest intent. On the other hand, if the communicator believes he only wants to convey information to increase understanding, but in truth his real (though unrecognized) intent is to demonstrate to another how much the communicator knows in order to enhance his own social status, this action would be classified as a latent intent. Latent intents, then, are those that are unintended and/or unrecognized.

Manifest and latent consequences can be seen in terms of the audience as well as the communicator. Wright cites the following:

5 | Message. 20 | Political Communication. 22 | Editorial/Editorializing. 24 | Advertising/Publicity. 25 | Public Relations.
26 | Propaganda. 32 | Mass Communication Activities. 58 | Content Analysis.

A local health campaign may be carried on for the purpose of persuading people to come to a clinic for a check-up. [This is the manifest, or intended activity.] While pursuing this goal, the campaign may have the unanticipated [latent] result of improving the morale of the local public health employees, whose everyday work has suddenly been given public attention. (Wright, 1959:17.)

Whether conscious or unconscious, communications do have thrusts: to persuade, to create empathy, to transmit information, to call attention to ourselves, etc. "It is difficult for many students of communications to comprehend the degree to which intention may modify the meaning of a given communication," says Gordon (1971:45), "in spite of the fact that most of us in informal situations either use statements of intentions to influence our actions, or imply intentions from others that we then construe as the content of what they are trying to communicate to us." An understanding of the communicator's intent, then, increases the effectiveness of communication.

Part Five

MASS MEDIA FUNCTIONS

32 | MAJOR MASS COMMUNICATION ACTIVITIES

FOUR MAJOR MASS communication activities (sometimes called functions) can be identified (Wright, 1959). These are: 1. Watching over the environment. 2. Helping the society respond to its environment. 3. Transmitting the social heritage to new members of the society. 4. Entertainment.

Watching over the environment. This refers to collecting and distributing information on events both outside and within the society. Lasswell (1948) terms this "surveillance of the environment." It is the news function of the press.

Helping the society respond to the environment. This involves (a) interpreting events in the environment, and (b) prescribing appropriate conduct in reaction to these events. Lasswell (1948) terms this "correlation of the parts of society in responding to the environment." This is popularly identified as editorial or propaganda activity.

Transmitting the social heritage. Commonly identified as educational activity, it is the communication of information, values, and social norms from one generation to another, from members of the society or group to newcomers.

Entertainment. This refers to communicative acts primarily intended for amusement.

Each of the four major mass communication activities may have desirable consequences in terms of the welfare of the society or its members. They may also have undesirable consequences, that is, they may prove "dysfunctional" for the society. For example, too much news may heighten anxieties, cause people to retreat to their private lives, or become apathetic. Interpretation of news by mass media may weaken people's critical faculties. Mass entertainment may discourage artistic creativity and excellence. (Merton, 1957.)

21 | News.   26 | Propaganda.   33 | Social Norm Function.
34 | Status-Conferral Function.   35 | Narcotizing Dysfunction.
36 | Privatization.   37 | Supplementation.   39 | Canalization.

PARTIAL FUNCTIONAL INVENTORY FOR MASS COMMUNICATIONS

System under Consideration

	Society	Individual	Specific Subgroups (e.g. Political Elite)	Culture
1. MASS-COMMUNICATED ACTIVITY: SURVEILLANCE (NEWS)				
Functions (manifest and latent)	Warning: Natural dangers; Attack; war. Instrumental: News essential to the economy and other institutions. Ethicizing	Warning; Instrumental. Adds prestige: Opinion leadership. Status conferral	Instrumental: Information useful to power. Detects: Knowledge of subversive and deviant behavior. Manages public opinion: Monitors, Controls. Legitimizes power: Status conferral	Aids cultural contact; Aids cultural growth
Dysfunctions (manifest and latent)	Threatens stability: News of "better" societies. Fosters panic	Anxiety; Privatization; Apathy; Narcotization	Threatens power: News of reality; "Enemy" propaganda; Exposés	Permits cultural invasion
2. MASS-COMMUNICATED ACTIVITY: CORRELATION (EDITORIAL SELECTION, INTERPRETATION, AND PRESCRIPTION)				
Functions (manifest and latent)	Aids mobilization; Impedes threats to social stability; Impedes panic	Provides efficiency: Assimilating news. Impedes: Overstimulation, Anxiety, Apathy, Privatization	Helps preserve power	Impedes cultural invasion; Maintains cultural consensus

	Society	Individual	Subgroups	Culture
Dysfunctions (manifest and latent)	Increases social conformism: Impedes social change if social criticism is avoided	Weakens critical faculties; Increases passivity	Increases responsibility	Impedes cultural growth

3. MASS-COMMUNICATED ACTIVITY: CULTURAL TRANSMISSION

	Society	Individual	Subgroups	Culture
Functions (manifest and latent)	Increases social cohesion: Widens base of common norms, experiences, etc.; Reduces anomie; Continues socialization: Reaches adults even after they have left such institutions as school	Aids integration: Exposure to common norms; Reduces idiosyncrasy; Reduces anomie	Extends power: Another agency for socialization	Standardizes; Maintains cultural consensus
Dysfunctions (manifest and latent)	Augments "mass" society	Depersonalizes acts of socialization		Reduces variety of subcultures

4. MASS-COMMUNICATED ACTIVITY: ENTERTAINMENT

	Society	Individual	Subgroups	Culture
Functions (manifest and latent)	Respite for masses	Respite	Extends power: Control over another area of life	
Dysfunctions (manifest and latent)	Diverts public: Avoids social action	Increases passivity; Lowers "tastes"; Permits escapism		Weakens aesthetics: "Popular culture"

From Charles R. Wright, "Functional Analysis and Mass Communication," in *Public Opinion Quarterly*, Vol. 24 (1960), pp. 605–620; for a recent and fuller statement of this functional approach see Wright's *Mass Communications: A Sociological Perspective*, 2nd ed. (New York: Random House, 1975).

33 | SOCIAL NORM FUNCTION

AS A SOCIETY changes from a traditional society to an industrial, complex society, the mass media take on an added function—the enforcement of social norms (sometimes called ethicizing). In this function, the mass media expose to public view deviations from established folkways, mores, and laws—and, hence, work toward a single morality.

> The mechanism of public exposure would seem to operate somewhat as follows. Many social norms prove inconvenient for individuals in the society. They militate against the gratification of wants and impulses. Since many find the norms burdensome, there is some measure of leniency in applying them both to oneself and to others. Hence, the emergence of deviant behavior and private toleration of these deviations. But this can continue only so long as one is not in a situation where one must take a public stand for or against the norms. Publicity, the enforced acknowledgment by members of the group that these deviations have occurred, requires each individual to take such a stand. He must either range himself with the non-conformists, thus proclaiming his repudiation of the group norms, and thus asserting that he, too, is outside the moral framework or, regardless of his private predilictions, he must fall into line by supporting the norm. Publicity closes the gap between "private attitudes" and "public morality." Publicity exerts pressure for a single rather than a dual morality by preventing continued evasion of the issue. It calls forth public reaffirmation and (however sporadic) application of the social norm. (Lazarsfeld and Merton, 1948:103.)

SOCIAL NORM FUNCTION

The following case history illustrates how the Social Norm Function operated in a small southern community once the "bright glare of publicity" was focused on the existence of minor gambling in a nearby resort establishment.

1964

Resort outside city limits installs five slot machines in a closed, upstairs room for play by selected guests.

1965–66

Within 18 months the presence of the slot machines is common knowledge in the surrounding area, despite laws against such activity. Only a small per cent of the population, however, play the machines.

1968

At a civic club meeting in late 1968, mayor is questioned about the adviseability of having the machines in the community, which is reported in local newspaper. The mayor (who, some say, plays the machines) now makes public declaration against machines, but says they are outside his jurisdiction.

1969

More letters-to-editor against gambling follow. Some civic and religious groups make call for action. When questioned in a public gathering, county commissioners make public stand in favor of current gambling laws.

1970

County attorney takes action. In short period of time, police close gaming room. Owner of resort is fined.

34 | STATUS-CONFERRAL FUNCTION

AS LAZARSFELD AND MERTON (1948) point out, the mass media can confer status upon issues, persons, organization, or social movements by singling them out for attention. The audiences of mass media apparently subscribe to the circular belief that if one really matters, he will be at the focus of mass media attention, and, if one is the focus of mass media attention, then one must really matter.

> The mass media bestow prestige and enhance the authority of individuals and groups by legitimizing their status. Recognition by the press testifies that one has arrived, that one is important enough to have been singled out from the large, anonymous masses, that one's behavior and opinions are significant enough to require public notice. (Lazarsfeld and Merton, 1948:101.)

It is this function of the press that has greatly contributed to the rise of the press agent, to much of the success of the student demonstrations of the twentieth century, and to the widespread use of some kinds of testimonials in certain advertising patterns, among others.

Many feel that the community press is successful in a mass society because it confers status on persons in its area who receive no attention in the national press or regional press. Thus such persons are aided in establishing an identity and finding a sense of community.

24 | Advertising/Publicity.   26 | Propaganda.   32 | Mass Communication Activities.   42 | Public Opinion.   48 | Mass Society/Mass Culture.

35 | NARCOTIZING DYSFUNCTION

THE NARCOTIZING dysfunction of the mass media centers itself on the human propensity to substitute knowing for doing.

It is the accumulation (from the mass media) of information concerning public issues, and the substitution of this awareness—or knowledge—for social action. This is often done on the assumption that since there is such awareness, some person (or group, or agency) must be taking some kind of action.

The narcotizing dysfunction works this way: Through contact with the mass media, an individual becomes an interested and informed citizen. This interested and informed citizen congratulates himself on this state of information and interest. He may even engage in considerable discussions on his informed topics with his friends, acquaintances, and relatives. Yet, all the while, he fails to see that he has abstained from decision and action. In short, like the workings of a narcotic, the individual is lulled into a false sense of security.

This process is viewed as dysfunctional rather than functional, say Lazarsfeld and Merton (1948:105), for it is "not in the interest of modern complex society to have large masses of the population politically apathetic and inert."

It is theorized that mass societies, such as the United States, could well have large segments of their population which could be labeled as informed and inert. Extensive networks of the mass media—newspapers, radio, magazines, television, motion pictures, and books—bombard the populace with information at every turn, at any hour of the day or night. This, coupled with the fact that basically individuals register their force and feelings in a mass society through interest groups and associations, tends to create conditions conducive to narcotization, it is felt.

42 | Public Opinion. 47 | Collective Excitement. 48 | Mass Society/Mass Culture.

36 | PRIVATIZATION

PRIVATIZATION IS THE shifting by an individual from existing group goals toward strictly personal goals. The individual's orientation is of a private, even autistic, nature. He is absorbed almost exclusively with his own comfort, safety, and personal security, whether his concern be physical, psychological, social, or financial.

In extreme states, privatization leads to panic. Fortunately, these extreme states are rarely encountered, and when they do occur, they do not persist for very long.

On the other hand, mild states of privatization are viewed by many theorists as a continuing condition among some members of a mass society as a result of the extensive networks of mass communication. This continuing state is seen this way: at any given time some people are overwhelmed by all the information coming to them from the news media. Lacking an ability to deal with it adequately, they turn their time and attention to matters in their private lives over which they do have a degree of control.

This relationship between the news media and privatization has been of concern to communication theorists for some time. The theorists see this retreat to private matters as dysfunctional behavior by these individuals; that is, it is not in the best interest of a society to have members of that society behave in such manner.

Privatization can also be the result of too little communication, particularly in its more extreme forms. As group communication is hampered, shared definitions diminish, opening the way to states of privatization. It has been noted that panic in battle might be avoided if the troops could talk to one another.

42 | Public Opinion. 47 | Collective Excitement. 48 | Mass Society/Mass Culture.

37 | SUPPLEMENTATION

SUPPLEMENTATION REFERS to the reinforcing interplay between the mass media and other sources of information, particularly interpersonal. Rather than a direct source for attitudinal or opinion formation or change, the media are viewed as playing an auxiliary role, supplementing the use of other, often organized communicative sources.

The concept of supplementation grew out of early communications research. For instance, a 1940 survey of the effects of the mass media on voting behavior suggested the media's auxiliary role. So, too, did an early study on a war bond drive. The evidence indicated a media channelling and supplementary influence. The results of a propaganda campaign to reduce racial prejudice sponsored by the United Nations also support this conclusion. McQuail (1969:46) concludes,

> There is indeed overwhelming evidence that the measured net changes in attitudes or opinion as a result of persuasive material, presented on radio, film, television or the press, are likely to be small. The large amount of detailed evidence which has accumulated has been formulated by Klapper (1960, p. 8) into a set of generalizations the most important of which states that: "Mass communication ordinarily do not serve as a necessary and sufficient cause of audience effects, but rather functions among and through a nexus of mediating influences."

Currently, among students of all types of communication, there is much discussion and debate on the extent to which the mass media are a direct influence and the extent to which they are an auxiliary influence. Certainly, studies on media influence have tended to focus on short-term, measurable effects. The results of such studies support the supplementation concept. Consequently, McQuail argues that, "Where all this weighty evidence could be misleading is in its neglect of the obvious, and in the tendency for an effect to be narrowly defined as a change due solely to some specific communication experience." The fact that the mass media are powerful

28 | Attitude/Opinion. 29 | Attitude Change. 42 | Public Opinion.
54 | Uses and Gratification Approach.

influences in some very evident ways can easily be lost sight of, he says.

Gordon (1969:289–90), also, reflects this position:

> To maintain, as most extant sociological research today does, that mass communications only "facilitate" current social attitudes and behaviors is, of course, on its face, absurd—largely because advertisers employing these technologies have *proved* their power for behavioral change beyond doubt. They have spent fortunes demonstrating in numerous ways that commercial messages of many kinds, spread by these techniques, change *all manner* of attitudes, aspirations, customs and even tastes. The commercial successes of their enterprises rest upon demonstrable cause and effect relationships between mass communications and behavior. The power of today's publicity and public relations organizations (or industrial and philanthropic propaganda arms) is further proof that many specific techniques of communication *work* in the nebulous business of modifying attitudes and opinions—and that they usually work quite efficiently.

Nevertheless, in many ways the mass media do fulfill the function of supplementation in persuasive communications. Berelson and Steiner (1964:532) note that since audience attention is self-selective exposure to communications in different media tends to be supplementary. That is, those who read about a topic also tend to listen; those who pay attention at one time also tend to pay attention at another time.

38 | MONOPOLIZATION

A CONDITION of monopolization exists when there is a control of the communicative acts which structures the situation so that the individual has no opportunity to weigh alternatives.

This condition can be said to exist when there is little or no opposition in the mass media to the diffusion of certain values, policies, or public images; that is, when there is an absence of counterpropaganda.

Monopolization is effective in a society because the beliefs and values that most of us hold are conditioned by our social environment. Our behavior is based on our perceptions; and the type of decisions we make are based on the information available to us. If one can control the social environment through monopolization, he can then manipulate the thinking and behavior of other people.

> Under a monopoly of mass communications, many members of the audience can be brought to change their opinions in the desired direction—but even here there are important qualifications: (a) by no means can all the members be brought to change their positions; (b) the process takes time; and (c) the monopoly must be complete or nearly complete; if it is not, enough communications will filter through to provide social support for the views of sizable numbers of people previously convinced of positions opposed to the monopolist's position. (Berelson and Steiner, 1964:531–532.)

On a societal basis, monopolization is most easily achieved in a totalitarian system. Here the necessary censorship can be exercised to ensure that only messages of a particular hue and color are transmitted. Consequently, people such as Hitler, Mussolini, Khrushchev, and Mao have been able to mold public opinion far more easily than has any propagandist in a democratic society where monopolization—on a societal level, at least—is much more difficult, if not impossible, to achieve.

39 | CANALIZATION

ONE OF THE major components in the broader area of study concerning the relationship between the mass media and attitude change is the concept of canalization. Canalizing refers to the mass media's ability to channel an individual's behavior patterns or attitudes.

On the one hand, the mass media can be instrumental in the formation of attitudes—the development of pro or con action tendencies on the part of an individual. The mass media can also be instrumental in the changing of attitudes—shifts in the action tendencies of the individual.

On the other hand, the media can canalize behavior, as opposed to the creating (formation) or reshaping (changing) of attitudes. That is to say, once the attitude has been formed, the media can act as an agent to direct it in one direction or another. An example of this phenomenon is offered by Lazarsfeld and Merton (1948) when they note that for Americans who have been socialized in the use of a toothbrush, it make relatively little difference which brand of toothbrush they use. The use of the toothbrush is, then, the formation of an action tendency on the part of the individual; the selection of one brand of toothbrush is the canalizing of that attitudinal behavior. Consequently, Lazarsfeld and Merton conclude that once the gross pattern of behavior or the generic attitude has been established, it can be canalized in one direction or another.

Some behavioral scientists view canalizing as a subdivision of attitude change; that is, what is normally referred to as change is a high-grade shift in behavior and what is referred to as canalizing is a low-grade shift in behavior.

40 | INOCULATION EFFECT

THE INOCULATION effect (or theory) in communications gets its name from its biological counterpart in creating a resistance to an unwanted condition. In this case, it is the procedure for making an individual or group resistant to counterpropaganda.

The analogy to the medical field is clear: an individual is injected with a mild amount of a virus; this virus, in turn, acts as a catalyst in creating a resistance to further inroads by the unwanted disease at a later time. The same process takes place in the communications field: an individual or group is exposed to (gets an injection of) a weakened amount of counterpropaganda (virus) which inoculates against the effects of later, and stronger, counterpropaganda (the disease).

The prominence of the inoculation effect in communications theory lies in the fact that there are two procedures for insulating an individual or group to counterattitudinal propaganda. One way is to make the attitude healthier by providing supportive information and arguments. (This is analogous to supportive therapy—going on a special diet, vitamins, and exercise regimen—to create biological resistance to disease.) The second way is to inoculate the attitudes by presenting the individual with weakened counterattitudinal propaganda (again as we inoculate for biological resistance). If the individual has been living in an environment where his attitudes have not been threatened, the inoculation procedure is the better of the two possible ways.

This "inoculation" is achieved by presenting a two-sided, as opposed to a one-sided, communication. In a two-sided presentation, the communicator does not concentrate solely on the points supporting the position he advocates, but rather he also discusses some of the opposing arguments as well. Apparently the two-sided argument prepares the listener to meet the counterarguments that may follow. As Lumsdaine and Janis (1953) point out, "In effect [the individual] has been given an advance basis for ignoring or discounting the opposing communication, and, thus 'inoculated,' he will tend to retain the [original] conclusion."

28 | Attitude/Opinion. 29 | Attitude Change. 59 | Communication Research.

Part Six

SOCIAL ENVIRONMENT FOR COMMUNICATIONS

41 | THEORIES OF THE PRESS

ACCORDING TO A school of thought widely held in democratic nations, there are four theories—or philosophies—of the relationship between the press and the society or government which it serves. They are: authoritarian, libertarian, Communist, and social responsibility (Siebert, Peterson, and Schramm, 1963).

Authoritarian. Under this concept, the press must support policies of the state. While the press is controlled by the government, such as by licenses or patents, it nevertheless functions as private enterprise.

After the invention of printing, royal governments adopted an authoritarian philosophy as they licensed the press in Europe. This theory forms the basis for press systems in many countries today, including Spain, Portugal, and several Latin American and Middle Eastern countries.

Libertarian. Under this system, the press functions to uncover and present truth to the people, operating chiefly as a private enterprise, and without government control. This philosophy is rooted in the ideas of Milton, Locke, and others that man has the right to pursue truth, that truth is best advanced when there is an "open market place of ideas."

The libertarian press is regulated by members of society, who may refuse to support certain newspapers or magazines, for example. The press serves as the informational link between the government and the people. Consequently, if information is restricted, then the people's right to be informed is denied.

Today the press of Great Britain and many other Western nations is largely based on this theory.

Communist. The press functions, under this philosophy, to perpetuate and expand the socialist system. It is simply an instrument of government, owned and used by the state.

16 | Mass Communication. 17 | Mass Media. 44 | Freedom of the Press. 45 | Censorship. 48 | Mass Society/Mass Culture.

The press is permitted and even encouraged to engage in self-criticism; for example, to criticize lesser bureaucrats' failure properly to fulfill their roles in the socialist state. But the criticism, whatever its nature, is closely controlled. The Soviet Communist theory is a development of the much older authoritarian theory.

Social Responsibility. An outgrowth of the libertarian theory, this philosophy places many moral and ethical restrictions on the press. It stresses "responsibility" instead of "freedom." For instance, due to the cost involved, most people cannot afford a mass medium to put forth their views in today's world. The social responsibility philosophy requires that the existing media offer avenues whereby these people's opinions can be heard.

Further, this theory views man not so much irrational as lethargic, and puts less faith than the libertarian theory on the idea that truth will rise from a clash of ideas.

The oldest of these philosophies is the authoritarian. It emerged in the authoritarian climate of the Renaissance, following the invention of printing. It was followed, in the 1700's and 1800's by the libertarian philosophy.

An understanding of the philosophy under which the press operates in a given society helps one to answer the question, "Why is the press in this society as it is?"—for the press, say Siebert, Peterson, and Schramm, always takes on the form and coloration of the social and political structures within which it operates. Especially does it reflect the system of social control whereby the relations of individuals and institutions are adjusted.

For a full discussion, see *Four Theories at the Press* by Siebert, Peterson, and Schramm. Also, see Merrill, *The Imperative of Freedom.*

FOUR RATIONALES FOR THE MASS MEDIA

	Authoritarian	Libertarian	Social Responsibility	Soviet-Totalitarian
Developed	in 16th and 17th century England; widely adopted and still practiced in many places	adopted by England after 1688, and in U.S.; influential elsewhere	in U.S. in the 20th century	in Soviet Union, although some of the same things were done by Nazis and Italians
Out of	philosophy of absolute power of monarch, his government, or both	writings of Milton, Locke, Mill, and general philosophy of rationalism and natural rights	writing of W. E. Hocking, Commission on Freedom of Press, and practitioners, media codes	Marxist-Leninist-Stalinist thought, with mixture of Hegel and 19th century Russian thinking
Chief purpose	to support and advance the policies of the government in power; and to service the state	to inform, entertain, sell—but chiefly to help discover truth, and to check on government	to inform, entertain, sell—but chiefly to raise conflict to the plane of discussion	to contribute to the success and continuance of the Soviet socialist system, and especially to the dictatorship of the party
Who has right to use media?	whoever gets royal patent or similar permission	anyone with economic means to do so	everyone who has something to say	loyal and orthodox party-members
How are media controlled?	government patents, guilds, licensing, sometimes censorship	by "self-righting process of truth" in "free market place of ideas," and by courts	community opinion, consumer action, professional ethics	surveillance and economic or political action of government
What forbidden?	criticism of political machinery and officials in power	defamation, obscenity, indecency, wartime sedition	serious invasion of recognized private rights and vital social interests	criticism of party objectives as distinguished from tactics
Ownership	private or public	chiefly private	private unless government has to take over to insure public service	public
Essential differences from others	instrument for effecting government policy, though not necessarily government owned	instrument for checking on government and meeting other needs of society	media must assume obligation of social responsibility; and if they do not, someone must see that they do	state-owned and closely controlled media existing solely as arm of state

From Fred S. Siebert, Theodore Peterson, and Wilbur Schramm, *Four Theories of the Press* (Urbana, Ill.: University of Illinois Press, 1963), p. 7.

42 | PUBLIC OPINION

THE TERM PUBLIC opinion is a very old one. Machiavelli, the 16th century Italian statesman, noted that a wise man will not ignore public opinion. The French social philosopher, de Tocqueville, surveyed American public opinion in a book published in Paris in 1835. The German sociologist, Tonnies, discussed the function of public opinion in 1887. Rousseau, in 1913, observed that in social change governments cannot be very far ahead of popular opinion, that governments rest on opinion rather than law or coercion.

In his classical work in 1922, Walter Lippmann delimited the concept public opinion, observing that a pattern of stereotypes largely determines what group of facts people see and in what light they see them. He concluded that public opinion is primarily a moralized and codified version of human preconceptions.

Early writers tended generally to comment about the mysterious, intangible nature of public opinion rather than define it. More recent observers have not hesitated in trying to define public opinion. Each, of course, has tended to see this concept according to his own perspective, to emphasize specific dimensions that another observer might ignore while including yet others. Thus there are about as many definitions as writers on the subject (Key, 1961:8).

Modern definitions tend to vary on these dimensions: (a) whether public opinion concerns a public issue; (b) whether opinion, to be pubic opinion, must be publicly expressed or may also be latent; (c) the degree of agreement required, or how many persons must share an opinion for it to be considered a public opinion; (d) whether an opinion must produce an effect of some kind to be considered a public opinion; and (e) whether the term opinion is synonymous with beliefs and values.

While many definitions of public opinion are very general, the concept would appear to be of only limited value unless it is delimited. Thus, with Best, we would recognize that public opinion is both an individual and mass phenomenon. Viewed as an individual phenomenon, one's expression of an opinion on a public concern is a public opinion, and such expression may help the individual cope with his environment. It may interest psychologists. But an individual opinion is not viewed as having much significance for society, government, or other large entities associated with the term public opinion. Public opinion more commonly is regarded as a mass phenomenon, as the aggregation and expression of individual opinions about a public concern, expressed in such manner as to be perceived by public decision makers. This is the public opinion that most concerns sociologists, political scientists, government officials, journalists, and others interested in the functioning of social groups and democratic, representative government (Best, 1973).

As a mass phenomenon, public opinion may be defined (partially in Hennessy's terms) as follows: Public opinion is the prevailing frame of mind—most often from an array of differing opinions—publicly expressed by a significant number of persons on an issue of public concern.

Let us consider the principal elements of this definition.

Prevailing frame of mind suggests the coming together of a significant number of private opinions as to distinguish this position from all other positions offered; hence to give public opinion the weight and force which it commands.

An array of differing opinions suggests that on any given issue there will be two or more, perhaps many, points of view. The term opinion suggests a verbal expression rather than a feeling, state, or deeply held religious or philosophical belief or value.

Publicly expressed means that this opinion is communicated in such manner as to come to the attention of public policy decision makers (as contrasted with those opinions privately held or shared within a small circle of friends with no communication beyond).

A significant number of persons suggests that enough individuals express the opinion to produce some effect—either through sheer numbers or the intensity with which they express opinions.

An issue of public concern means a contemporary situation of concern to many persons and concerning which there is a likelihood of disagreement. This rules out noncontroversial matters on which there is unanimity of opinion such as man's need for air and water, and nonsignificant matters such as whether or not gentlemen prefer blondes or brunettes. The term *issue* suggests that alternative judgments are possible, that opinions are still being entertained, that the questioned is not settled (Hennessy, 1970:25–30).

Public opinion often is described in terms of intensity and direction. Intensity indicates how strongly people express opinions on an issue. Direction indicates the flavor of their opinion, i.e., whether they favor, disfavor, or are neutral about an issue.

Public opinion must have a certain persistence as well as volume (number of persons among whom the opinion is diffused) to rank as public opinion. It is both permanent and transitory. Older opinions are resistant to change. Newer ones are more unstable, representing an ever shifting alignment.

One school of thought says that, within a collectivity, a simple majority of opinion is insufficient to constitute public opinion. At the same time, neither unanimity nor consensus is required. Public opinion, forever ebbing and flowing like the tide, is that weight of opinion found somewhere between majority and consensus that the resisting minority feel bound, not by fear but by conviction, to accept (Lang and Lang, 1967:372–374).

By some who work in the field, public opinion is also classified into manifest (or actual) and latent categories. They see *manifest public opinion* as public opinion that is evident—that is, the behavior of people, reacting to an issue, is observable. In contrast, they see *latent public opinion* as that public opinion which is anticipated before the issue arises, as well as opinions that have not yet crystallized. Much of what is not done, they say, is not done because of anticipated reaction to it.

43 | PUBLIC OPINION PROCESS

THE PUBLIC opinion process involves two elements. One, the public opinion situation, and, two, the product of this situation, public opinion.

Public Opinion Situation. As the schema shows, in its time sequence, the public opinion situation begins with the (1) already present mass sentiment of a society. (The basis of mass sentiment is to be found in the culture of the people, but this does not mean that mass sentiment and culture are the same.) When, (2) an issue or matter about which people have differing views is interjected into society, the people concerned begin to form (3) a public. Now, in a democracy, the critical part of the public opinion process develops. This is the (4) debate stage. What is central in this stage is the public discussion. However, the debate stage also includes propaganda, publicity, staged events, published polls—all the things that help shape opinion. The basis for this public discussion is the mass sentiment of the people; but just as the mass sentiment shapes the discussion it is in turn shaped by the discussion. During this debate period a certain (5) length of time must elapse which will insure that adequate debate has taken place. If it does not, the public is often left with the feeling that certain social action, based on the issue, was "railroaded through."

Public Opinion. After an adequate debate period has taken place, the result is (6) public opinion. Or as some call it, true public opinion. Or as some call it, informed public opinion. Now, one last step remains: the (7) denouement of the issue. Usually after some social action has taken place the issue is replaced by another issue. In some instances the product of the public opinion situation—public opinion—is so heavily in favor (near consensus) of one position that this position becomes a (8) societal value and takes its place as part of the mass sentiment; hence, completing a circle.

For a fuller discussion, see Lang and Lang, *Collective Dynamics.*

26 | Propaganda. 28 | Attitude/Opinion. 32 | Mass Communication Activities. 42 | Public Opinion. 48 | Mass Society/Mass Culture.

PUBLIC OPINION PROCESS

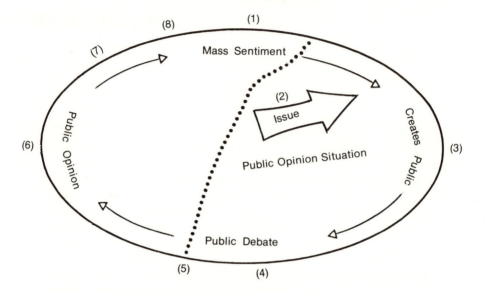

Social security provides an example of the public opinion process. Out of the mass sentiment that said that a society should provide for its aged, came the concept of social security. When this idea was put before the American people it became an issue and created its own public. This public debated the issue of social security within the framework of the mass sentiments. At a point in time, social legislation was enacted, based on the public opinion resulting from public debate. In time the concept became accepted by the bulk of the American people as a proper course of action; consequently, it took its place in the mass sentiment of the society. Today social security is no longer debatable, that is, it is no longer an issue. (The *concept* is no longer an issue, as some politicians have discovered; the *form* it should take, however, is an issue, in some circles.)

44 | FREEDOM OF THE PRESS

FREEDOM OF THE press generally is taken to mean freedom to disseminate information and ideas through the mass media without government restriction.

This concept evolved late in history, after a struggle against authority. Yet, even today the media are severely restricted in many countries.

In the United States, freedom of the press has been an accepted principle since Colonial days. It is formally guaranteed by the First Amendment to the Constitution. This states that "Congress shall make no law abridging the freedom of speech or the press."

The Supreme Court first applied the free press guarantee of the First Amendment to states in 1931, when it ruled as unconstitutional a Minnesota "gag law" permitting suppression of malicious and scandalous publication (Emery, Ault & Agee, 1965:43).

However, the First Amendment does not protect the press against attempted or actual restrictions or interference by economic, social, religious, or other non-governmental interests or pressures.

Freedom of the press is justified on several grounds: (a) as a protection against political tyranny, (b) as a vehicle for advancing truth, (c) as a "fourth branch of government," that is, to make democratic government work (Mill, 1869; Hudon, 1963; Chafee, 1947; Gerald, 1963).

But freedom of the press is not absolute. It must be limited where national survival is threatened or where press freedom conflicts with other constitutional rights, such as the right of an accused to be tried by an impartial jury (Hook, 1962).

In attempting to define the proper limits on a free press, U.S. courts and others have used various criteria over recent decades (Konvitz, 1963; Thomas, 1954; Hudon, 1963). These include:

(a) Protecting public utterances, but not private ones.
(b) Protecting expression of ideas, but not criminal acts.
(c) Protecting "liberty" but not "license"—a distinction, however, some find hard to establish clearly.

17 | Mass Media.   41 | Theories of the Press.   45 | Censorship.

(d) Protecting expression unless there is a "clear and present danger" that it will bring "substantive evils that Congress has a right to prevent."

(e) Balancing the various interests involved in determining whether to limit expression.

The "clear and present danger" doctrine was first enunciated by Justice Holmes in 1919. He argued that speech may on occasion be a form of action, noting that "the most stringent protection of free speech would not protect a man in falsely shouting 'fire' in a theater and causing a panic." Holmes observed that such an utterance, like a murderous act, may be forbidden by statute. However, this criterion was sharply criticized by libertarians—and eventually modified.

In Meiklejohn's view, application of the clear and present danger idea led to the annulment rather than the interpretation of the First Amendment. He argued that it failed to take into account the Constitutional distinction between *speech*, which Congress may limit, and *freedom of speech*, which it may not. Thus, for example, at a town meeting, a moderator may limit when persons may speak and impose other conditions to maintain order and permit the body to act on matters of common concern. But he cannot deny the expression of an idea because it is on one side of an issue rather than another. Thus, though citizens may, on other grounds be barred from speaking, they may not be barred because their views are thought to be false or dangerous (Meiklejohn, 1965:24, 27, 33, 49).

The clear and present danger test was later modified with stress placed on the notion that only in an emergency, when there is no opportunity for various ideas to be discussed, can speech be abridged. Thus, for example, when the roof falls in, the moderator, without violating the First Amendment, may declare the meeting adjourned. Since 1951 the doctrine has been largely abandoned.

The Supreme Court has constantly shifted its position on freedom of expression and has failed to formulate a coherent theory of the First Amendment. This has left the lower courts, public officials and private citizens confused over applicable rules.

In recent years the court has generally decided cases on an ad hoc basis, balancing interests, the only rationale acceptable to a majority of the justices, in solving the numerous First Amendment problems. But, says Emerson, in the hands of most judges, the balancing comes to be nothing more than a way of rationalizing preformed conclusions (Emerson, 1970:717–718).

Also concern has increased over the problem of assuring that criminal defendants are given a fair trial under the Sixth Amendment while at the same time preserving the First Amendment guarantees of a Free Press.

Noting increasing appeals from criminal convictions based on alleged prejudicial publicity, the American Bar Association in 1966 adopted the so-called Reardon rules governing what information lawyers, court and law enforcement officers may release to the press.

The bar and the news media in a considerable number of states and cities have entered into voluntary agreements on fair trial-free press principles. However, the American Newspaper Publishers Association, after a two-year study of the matter, concluded that the problem of pre-trial publicity has been greatly exaggerated. It declared that there are "grave inherent dangers to the public in the restriction or censorship at the source of news, among them secret arrest and ultimately secret trial."

Meanwhile, the application of First Amendment protection to sexual material has fluctuated with the changing makeup of the U.S. Supreme Court. In 1957, in the Roth case, the court ruled that the test of whether material is obscene and thus not entitled to protection is whether it deals with sex in a manner appealing to prurient interest. However, in 1966, the court ruled that for material to be found obscene, a showing had to be made that (a) the dominant theme of the material taken as a whole appeals to a prurient interest in sex; (b) the material is patently offensive because it affronts contemporary community standards relating to the description or representation of sexual matters; and (c) the material is utterly without redeeming social value. But in 1973, the court veered back to the right, holding that such material can be regulated by states, subject to specific safeguards, without a showing that it is utterly without redeeming social value. The court ruled that obscenity is to be determined by applying contemporary community standards.

In the 1970's the press and working newsmen frequently cited the First Amendment guarantees in defending their performance from attacks by government and other groups. In 1971, the U.S. House of Representatives, by a 226–181 vote, finally erased a contempt citation against CBS President Frank Stanton after the network refused to turn over to a House subcommittee subpoenaed materials used in producing the controversial film documentary, "The Selling of the Pentagon." The same year the Supreme court ruled in a 6–3 decision that the *New York Times* and the *Washington Post* could continue publishing the classified Pentagon papers dealing with the origins of the Vietnam war.

45 | CENSORSHIP

CENSORSHIP IS the deliberate exclusion of material from the flow of information in order to shape the opinion and actions of others.

This deliberate exclusion can take two forms. Censorship, in its narrowest sense, is the examination by an authority of messages intended for mass dissemination in order to suppress material objectionable to that authority. It is prior restraint, action to prevent dissemination of material. For example, it may involve cutting out certain words, phrases, or sentences by a censor.

More broadly, censorship may be taken to include any effort to discourage or prevent the dissemination of material objectionable to some authority. Thus, a government may withhold information or news which could reflect adversely upon its officials, or it may grant licenses in such manner as to discourage the dissemination of objectionable matter. Also, the authority may take punitive action against offenders (a) to guarantee that they do not offend again, and (b) to discourage others from disseminating objectionable material. Thus, newsprint may be withheld from certain publications, heavy taxes or other economic sanctions imposed, editors jailed, or broadcast licenses revoked.

Totalitarian governments use censorship to maintain their power. But because of traditions abhoring censorship, democratic governments must rely on other methods to stay in office—such as trying to win the honest support of influential media or taking their case directly to the people.

Censorship has been rare in the United States, except at the local level where there has been much action taken, aimed at alleged obscenity in printed material and motion pictures.

Managed News. There is also a lesser form of censorship that has come to be called managed news. This is the distribution of information in a manner that most benefits the distributor. Governments, corporations, and other bureaucracies are most often guilty of managed news.

32 | Mass Communication Activities. 42 | Public Opinion. 44 | Freedom of the Press.

Extra Legal Censorship. Extra legal censorship is that which is beyond legal control or authority. Such censorship may be voluntary, as when an editor eliminates a phrase or a word from a manuscript because he feels it is in bad taste, or a librarian takes a book out of circulation because she feels it is obscene and she dislikes obscene materials.

In one sense, extra legal censorship may sometimes be involuntary, as when in response to economic, political or other pressures. For example, a broadcast station may mute its criticism of government officials under real or perceived threats from such officials to its license renewal.

The movie industry has experienced both legal and extra-legal censorship. In 1907, the city of Chicago passed an ordinance under which police prescreened movies to determine if they were suitable for showing, and later several states set up review boards to censor movies.

In an effort to counter this trend toward legal censorship, the motion picture industry practiced self-censorship for several decades. The Motion Picture Association of America (MPAA), headed by Will Hays, reviewed films as they were completed and gave a seal of approval to those conforming to the MPAA's rather strict code. This code banned nudity, sensuality, foul language and the demeaning of religion, religious and national groups, and limited violence which could be shown in movies.

However, as television developed and gained popularity, the movie industry fell on hard times. Moreover, under a 1948 U.S. Supreme Court ruling, the movie studios had to divest themselves of theaters, and this undermined the enforcement of the code. At the same time, movies of the Hays era were criticized for lacking realism and content, and more realistic and daring foreign films became increasingly popular. Thus, the Hays code was liberalized in the 1950's and 1960's. In 1965, the Supreme Court severely restricted the application of prior censorship. Thus freed, movie makers found it handsomely profitable to exploit sex and violence. The result was a flood of movies depicting explicit sex, rape, abortion, and wholesale violence.

With legal censorship virtually dead, private groups such as the National Catholic Office of Motion Pictures, the Film Board of National Organizations (ten national organizations concerned about film content) and other groups continued to review and rate movies to alert parents and other citizens as to the content of new movies.

Finally, in 1968, the movie industry abandoned its code and instituted a rating system. As later revised, the ratings are:

G — All ages admitted.

PG — All ages admitted, but parental guidance is recommended.

R — Anyone under 17 must be accompanied by a parent or legal guardian.

X — No one under 18 admitted.

(Liston, 1973:40–53.)

46 | GATEKEEPER

A GATEKEEPER is a person who, whether interacting within the formal or the informal channels of communication, can determine *if* and *how* a message will be transmitted. By this definition all members of the community are, at least to some degree, gatekeepers. As Schramm (1960:170) notes:

> . . . At every point along the chain, someone has the right to say whether the message shall be received and retransmitted, and whether it shall be retransmitted in the same form or with changes. In other words, all along the chain are a series of *gatekeepers,* who have the right to open or close the gate to any message that comes along.

The term gatekeeper was first used by the social scientist Kurt Lewin. He noted that how a news item travels through communications channels depends on the "gates" in these channels, that these gates are controlled either by impartial rules or "gatekeepers" (White, 1950:383).

The gatekeeper, Schramm says, plays one of the most important roles in social communication today, and a "few important gatekeepers have an enormous power over our views of our environment." As a result, communication research has tended to focus on those gatekeepers in both the formal and informal channels who have a higher message contact rate than does the average participant. In the informal systems, these gatekeepers are the central communicators in rumor systems, and the influentials in the interpersonal networks; in the formal channels these gatekeepers are reporters, news editors, wire editors, and the like in the mass media, and department heads, division heads, chairmen, etc., in the formal organizations. In short, they are the gatekeepers in all channels who are at the same time making more *decisions* and *more important* decisions concerning the flow of news.

Gatekeepers in the informal channels of communication are

drawn equally from both sexes, and crosscut all social categories such as age, income, social status, etc. On the other hand, gatekeepers in the formal channels of communication tend to be in their critical positions because of a certain expertise which they bring to their work; these gatekeepers tend to be male, and have higher education, income, etc., than their contemporaries.

How gatekeepers operate can be demonstrated in the news business. Initially, assignment editors decide which of the vast number of human events and activities should be reported. They do this with one eye on the newspaper's columns of news space or the broadcast station's air time available for reporting news. They assign reporters to cover these events, although the reporters themselves frequently suggest assignments as they pick up leads on events they judge to be worthy of reporting and/or of interest to them personally. These reporters, in turn, serve as other gatekeepers. They make numerous decisions as to which facts they should dig out and report, just how they are to write their reports. Ideally, they write balanced, accurate, and unbiased accounts of original events, but admittedly their accounts are affected to some degree by the reporters' own biases. Next, their copy is given to other gatekeepers in the newspaper editorial rooms or broadcast news rooms. These men and women may delete certain paragraphs or sentences or words, they may pass the story exactly as originally written, or they may throw it out altogether—the latter situation frequently because there is no room for the story left in the paper or on the newscast.

Sometimes gatekeeper editors may decide that an event is really not news, but later change their minds. Seymour Hersh, former Associated Press Pentagon writer who broke the story of the infamous My Lai massacre in Vietnam, claims that gatekeeper editors at first ignored this story (Hersh, 1972:434).

In aggregate, gatekeepers discard vast amounts of news material that could be published or broadcast. One study shows that a typical state Associated Press Bureau (Wisconsin) received 57,000 words or 283 news items a day, and transmitted to non-metropolitan daily papers in the state an average of 19,423 words or 122 items (including locally originated copy). Of this, the average non-metropolitan newspaper used only 12,848 words or 74 items (Cutlip, 1954:436).

47 | COLLECTIVE EXCITEMENT

COLLECTIVE EXCITEMENT is the state of tension existing in a public. This public can be as large as to embrace an entire society, as when one country goes to war with another, or as small as some social group, as when a fraternity becomes a public to a college activity.

The prevailing state of collective excitement has a direct bearing on both the nature and frequency of message transmission. Collective excitement is usually divided into three types:

High collective excitement. This state of tension is characterized by conditions of disaster, impending disaster, or great success. The consequences of events that make for high collective excitement are far-reaching and unpredictable.

Moderate collective excitement. This state of tension is characterized by conditions of widespread interest or concern that is beyond usual interest because of minor consequential and problematic aspects.

Low collective excitement. This state of tension is characterized as the continuing state of interest in usual day-to-day activities, as social man goes about keeping his bearings in a highly complex and changing world.

Central to the study of collective excitement is the part played by the formal and informal channels of communication. For instance, in times of high collective excitement, the demand for news is high. Members of the public simply do not get enough news about their focus of interest. Hence, both formal and informal channels are utilized at an accelerated rate. In contrast, in times of low collective excitement, the demand for news is low. Formal channels of communication tend to provide sufficient information to interested publics to reduce the gap between that which is demanded and what is provided.

The accompanying schema indicates the conditions put upon the

8 | Informal Channels of Communication. 14 | Rumor. 16 | Mass Communication.

111

transmission of news through informal channels (conceptualized as rumor) by the three stages of collective excitement. It points up that in message dissemination in these channels the conditions surrounding transmission are as important as the message content. For fuller elaboration in this area, see Tamotsu Shibutani's *Improvised News: A Sociological Study of Rumor.*

COLLECTIVE EXCITEMENT AND RUMOR CONSTRUCTION

	Unsatisfied Demand For News	Level of Verified News	Degree of Formalization in Social Interactions	Speed of Rumor Construction	Formation of Rumor
High Collective Excitement	High	Low	Low Relaxation of conventional norms governing social distance, source of information, verification procedures, and subject matter	High Limited only by physical barriers	Often takes place in spontaneously formed channels
Moderate Collective Excitement	Moderate	Moderate	Moderate Only a mild relaxation of conventional norms	Moderate Limited by the available communication channels and degree of formalization	Mainly limited to auxiliary channels; some rumor construction will take place in spontaneously formed channels; distinguished by deliberative process in rumor construction
Low Collective Excitement	Low	High	High Shared understandings concerning who may address whom about what subject, under what circumstances, and with what degree of confidence	Low Normal barriers to social intercourse	Takes place in auxiliary channels

From Reed H. Blake, "The Relationship Between Collective Excitement and Rumor Construction," in *The Rocky Mountain Social Science Journal*, Vol. 6, No. 2 (1969), pp. 119–126.

COLLECTIVE EXCITEMENT AND RUMOR CONSTRUCTION (cont.)

	Content of Rumor	Sample Conditions	Societies Conducive to Level of Excitement	Impact of Mass Media Availability to Levels of Excitement
High Collective Excitement	Rumor is expressive of emotional dispositions shared by some portion of the public; may be inconsistent with cultural axioms	Natural disasters of major import: floods, earthquakes, fires, etc.; acts of war: invasions, bombings, etc.; acts of civil disobedience: large scale rioting, looting, etc., insurrections	Mass. Conditions of mass society conducive to circular effect between high collective excitement and high degree of unsatisfied demand for news	The increased communicative acts available to a society by the presence of the mass media work to reduce rumor construction as well as to create conditions for emotional contagion; the latter, in turn, works toward a circular effect of high collective excitement
Moderate Collective Excitement	Some distortion from cultural axioms	Political and economic decisions of widespread consequence; minor natural disasters; acts of civil disobedience minor in nature	Transitory. Conditions of transitory societies conducive to moderate collective excitement and to moderate degree of unsatisfied demand for news	In times of moderate collective excitement, mass media can usually meet the demand for verified news; if lines of formal channels are severed, however, the resulting vacuum could work toward high collective excitement
Low Collective Excitement	Rumor content is plausible, consistent with cultural axioms	Decisions, acts of natural forces of some social import; day-to-day living	Traditional. The stable conditions of traditional societies are conducive to low collective excitement and to a low degree of unsatisfied demand for news	In times of low collective excitement, mass media work to reduce the level of rumor construction

48 | MASS SOCIETY/ MASS CULTURE

MASS SOCIETY has been called a creation of the modern age and a product of the division of labor, of mass communication, and a more or less democratically achieved consensus (Wirth, 1948).

A mass society is characterized by the following general conditions:

1. A mass society involves large masses of people, numbering even into the hundreds of millions.

2. The members of a mass society are dispersed over wide areas, instead of being concentrated into compact local groups.

3. A mass society is strongly influenced by powerful bureaucratic organizations.

4. The social structure of a mass society is equalitarian in theory, if not in practice.

5. A mass society is heterogeneous in religion, ethnic background, style of life, and access to positions of power.

6. Members of a mass society respond to, and are participants in, the phenomena of mass culture.

7. Members of a mass society are anonymous individuals, who know others within their local social groups, but not other members, most often removed in space, in the mass society.

8. Except in such rare cases as mobilization for war, members of a mass society seldom form an organized group.

9. Members of a mass society are all—to some degree—alienated from society itself by lack of adequate access to the primary relationships available to members of more traditional societies.

10. Mass society is secular, its members having less veneration for tradition than do members of older societies.

11. A mass society has undergone a complex technological development.

12. Finally, an important part of the interaction in a mass society occurs through the process of mass communication.

16 | Mass Communication. 17 | Mass Media. 32 | Mass Communication Activities.

Irrespective of the form of government, mass societies are found in Europe, Asia, and America. And the members of these mass societies exert their influence on the larger society—not as individuals—but as members of interest groups, or organizations.

Mass culture is a set of shared ideas and behavior patterns that cross-cuts socio-economic lines and subcultural groupings within a complex society. These commonly shared ideas and behavior patterns serve as points of reference and identification for members of the society. By many, then, mass culture is viewed as a kind of least common denominator, and as a kind of film hiding the diversity beneath (Bennett and Tumin, 1948:609).

Mass culture is made possible by mass communication (which is the agent that gets before large numbers of people the common ideas and behavior, and reinforces these patterns, as well) and by mass transportation (which delivers the cultural artifacts—in the form of "fashionable" clothing, film, recordings, furniture, etc.—for mass consumption).

Mass culture is often referred to as popular culture. Himes (1968) using music as an example, makes the distinction between mass culture and other major strains of the cultural heritage. He notes that classical and true folk music, on the one hand, does not depend upon mass communication for its development. But popular music, on the other hand, is dependent upon the mass media for its existence.

Examples of mass cultural artifacts are TV dinners, drive-in movies, slang, do-it-yourself kits, dating, slogans, rock music festivals, baseball, bubble gum, diet plans, lithographed pictures, and most current styles in clothing, home furnishings, and automobiles—in short, products manufactured solely for a mass market.

Mass culture can be contrasted with high culture (elite culture, superior culture, or refined culture). High culture includes what are conceived as the great works of poetry, music, writing, philosophy, painting, sculpture, drama, architecture, craftsmanship, and the like.

Summarizing Ernest Van Den Haag, the following characteristics of mass culture are offered by Gordon (1969:293):

1. Production and consumption of culture are separated; culture is primarily a spectator sport.

2. Mass production standardizes a product to please average tastes and these tastes determine the nature of the output.

3. Power to bestow prestige and success rests with the masses rather than a cultural elite; high culture is interesting only as gossip concerning celebrated artists, i.e., *TV Guide*, and *Life* on Horowitz and Picasso.

4. The mass requires distraction from life: thrills, sentimentality and escapism; the bulk of mass culture deals in these qualities.

5. Popularity and popular approval become the dominant moral and aesthetic standards in art and subsequently in life itself.

6. The lure of mass markets diverts potential talent from the creation of art; because commercial artists know this, they lament their "sellout" to the "cult of the golden calf."

7. Excessive communication tends to isolate people from one another and from real experience; fabricated experiences (Judy Garland's "concerts," for instance) are "realer" than life—almost spiritual—for many.

8. Since mass culture serves average tastes, it tends to reshape all art—past and present—to meet the expectations and demands of the masses; one discovers hippie *Hamlets* and reads from front page articles on fantastic prices paid for "great" paintings.

9. The total effect of mass culture is to militate against the individual's confrontation with a potential life of boredom.

Gordon draws our attention to the fact that this notion of mass culture is not deeply concerned with the artistic quality of the communications which constitute the fabric of mass culture, merely that it is standardized, average, escapist, etc., all characteristics which relate to the psychologics of the instruments involved rather than their logics of aesthetics.

A major aspect of mass culture is mass entertainment. *Mass entertainment* is entertainment derived from the mass media of communication: the experiencing of pleasure via television, radio, the cinema, popular novels, newspapers, and magazines (Mendelsohn, 1966:15).

The designation of entertainment as mass entertainment is centered on two aspects:

1. The attempt to attract as large an audience as possible. This appeal to many social-economic groupings produces a heterogeneous audience; hence, producers of mass entertainment place emphasis upon exploitation of common denominators of shared tastes within this "mass." An example is the exploitation of human emotion by mass media.

2. The term "entertainment" is meant that activity which provides pleasurable diversion irrespective of any social message or value that may be associated with it.

From a sociological perspective, mass entertainment is an escape hatch from the local community as well as from immediate social pressures. It is an entrance to the larger world in which one can participate, to which one is welcome, and in which one can, in a sense, consort with the well-known (Burns, 1967).

In contemporary United States, as well as many other countries such as Japan, Germany, and England, nearly everyone is entertained to some extent by the mass media; almost everyone listens to radio, watches television, reads magazines and newspapers, or attends motion picture theatres. Thus, mass entertainment as a form of social activity represents a behavioral manifestation that is nearly universal. Further, there is evidence to suggest that people participate more in mass entertainment as they become more affluent (Mendelsohn, 1966).

Part Seven

INVESTIGATIVE APPROACHES AND TOOLS

49 | INDIVIDUAL DIFFERENCES THEORY

AN OUTGROWTH of the mechanistic stimulus-response (S-R) thinking of early psychological activity, the individual differences theory of mass communication views members of an audience as distinct and separate individuals who will, upon giving attention to a message, handle it in ways distinct to themselves (rather than as a uniform audience member).

DeFleur (1966:121), in his delineation of this theory, cites the fundamental postulates of this approach:

1. Human beings vary greatly in their personal psychological organization.

2. In part, these variations begin with a differential biological endowment, but are also due, in greater measure, to differential learning.

3. Human beings raised under widely differing circumstances are exposed to widely differing points of view.

4. From these learning environments they acquire a set of attitudes, values, and beliefs that constitute their personal psychological make-up and set each somewhat apart from the other.

The key concept, then, in this formulation is *conditioning*.

Consequently, the processes of selective exposure and selective retention—major conceptions in the field of psychology—play central roles in this theory. That is to say, different types of people in an audience *select* and *interpret* mass-communicated messages in different types of ways.

In summary, DeFleur concludes:

> The individual differences theory of mass communication implies that media messages contain particular stimulus attributes that have differential interaction with personality characteristics of members of the audience. Since there are individual differences in personality characteristics among such members, it is natural to assume that there will be variations in effect which correspond to

such individual differences. However, by holding constant the mediating influences of personality variables (that is by considering people with similar personality characteristics), such a theory would still predict uniformity of response to a given message (if the intervening variables operate uniformally). Thus, the logical structure of the individual differences theory is a "cause-(intervening process)-effect" structure, just as was the mechanistic S-R theory before it. (DeFleur, 1966:122.)

50 | SOCIAL CATEGORIES THEORY

THE SOCIAL categories theory of mass communication states that people with similar social characteristics will display similar mass communication behavior. This behavior includes media exposure, media preference, communication effects, and the like.

The major social characteristics involved in this phenomenon are education, income, occupation, race/ethnic, religion, age, sex, and geographic location.

> The underlying assumption [of the social categories theory is] that, in spite of the great diversity of modern society, audience members who have similar social characteristics will share common orientations and patterns of usage concerning the mass media. Such a formulation is more descriptive than explanatory, but it is undoubtedly true that people who have similar attributes relate themselves to the media in roughly similar ways. For this reason, the influence of social categories on the mass communication process remains an important consideration. (DeFleur, 1971:419.)

Indeed, since the late 1930's, much of the sociologist's interest in communication studies have been centered in social categories theory.

Today the magazine world is predominately geared to the social categories theory in its publishing output. In fact, the general magazine has almost totally disappeared from the American scene. Instead, magazines are geared for specific audiences, most often described by one or more social characteristics—witness *Seventeen, Sunset, Outdoor Life, Better Homes and Gardens*, among others.

Radio, too, has (with the advent of television) more recently gone the social categories route in its programming. Here are found stations whose music, news, sports, and talk are designed to attract listeners from particular social categories (or configurations of categories).

One can also point to evidence of social categories theory in the other media. Indeed, many behavioral scientists feel that all media will be catering to specific audiences in the not-to-distant-future.

51 | TWO-STEP FLOW OF COMMUNICATION THEORY

THE TWO-STEP flow, according to the Lazarsfeld, Berelson, and Gaudet study, The Peoples' Choice, offers the hypothesis that mass-communicated messages do not always reach all members of their ultimate audience directly. Sometimes through a two-step process, the messages first reach one segment of society and then are passed on to others:

The strength of the two-step flow theory is that it takes into account the fact that man is not a social isolate but is an active participant in many primary and secondary interpersonal relationships. Thus, rather than viewing mass media effectiveness as solely a result of direct influence on the audience, the two-step theory suggests that information often flows from the mass media to influentials (or opinion leaders) and from them to their less-active associates for whom they are influential.

The rationale behind the two-step flow is that each individual is a member of many groups, formal and informal. As the individual interacts within these groups he is affected by them, and these groups exercise a great influence on his opinions and attitudes. Further, in many instances, these same individuals, at the time of their media exposure, are participating in group experiences. Consequently, while this theory emphasizes interpersonal relationships as (1) channels of information, it also draws attention to the fact that these same relationships (2) can serve as sources of pressure to conform to the group's way of thinking and acting, and (3) offer a foundation of social support for the individual.

Central to the two-step flow concept is the influential and his social characteristics. These characteristics are discussed elsewhere in this book. Yet it should be noted here that the influential and his influencees are very much alike, and typically belong to the same primary groups of family, friends, and associates. Also, while the influential is typically more interested in the particular sphere in which he is influential, it is unlikely that the influencees will be very far behind in their levels of interest.

Finally, despite his greater involvement with the mass media, the influential is also affected by still other people. This indicates that the flow of influence is not limited to just two steps; in any situation there could well be more than two steps.

Wright (1959:117) reminds us that the analysis of opinion leaders and the two-step flow are based primarily on studies on American audiences and that the extent to which one can generalize to other groups is as yet not fully explored. And even within our own society, Wright says, there is much still to be learned about the conditions under which the two-step flow operates—how prevalent it is among various minority groups, at different age levels, and in times of historical crisis.

52 | INFLUENTIALS

INFLUENTIALS, OR OPINION LEADERS, are the informed and trusted individuals in the community who, through day-to-day personal contacts in the primary group setting, influence others in matters of decision and opinion formation.

Since influentials interact with their peer groups, each stratum of society has its own corps of influentials.

The same individuals are not influential in every area of human activity—sports, politics, or fashions, for example. But they all channel the impersonal content of mass communication into interpersonal networks. And in doing this they introduce their own attitudes toward and evaluations of that content.

The effectiveness of the influential hinges on several factors: (1) since he is a member of the peer group, he is viewed as not representing a vested interest; hence, he is trusted; (2) in the face-to-face contact with influences, he can adjust the message to each individual; (3) in like manner, he can personally and immediately reward those who agree with him.

The influential is like—yet unlike—his influencee in several respects. Thus the influential has a much higher contact rate with the mass media, has a slightly higher income, has a higher level of education, is more socially gregarious, and is more venturesome than his followers. But the differences are not too great.

Two major kinds of influentials have been identified, local and cosmopolitan. The chief criterion for identifying the two types is the orientation toward community affairs. The cosmopolitan influential is relatively more concerned with the larger world, with national and international matters; the local influential is tied more to local and regional matters.

There are similarities and differences between the local and cosmopolitan influential:

The local influential is more likely to be a native son, the cosmopolitan more mobile. The local influential is more concerned with

8 | Informal Channels of Communication.   16 | Mass Communication.   51 | Two-Step Flow Theory. 53 | Adoption Curve.

knowing a large number of community members, while the cosmopolitan is more restrictive in his associations, tending to form friends with people with similar social rankings. Both types use the mass media more than does the average person in their community, but they differ in their communication selection and the uses to which they put the selected communication content: The localite favors hometown newspapers and straight news stories from the broadcast media; the cosmopolitan favors national and news magazines, metropolitan newspapers, and, from the broadcast media, the more interpretative newscasts provided by news commentators and analysts.

Further, the local influential's influence is polymorphic: his connections in the community—upon which rests his influence—cover several fields; he can exert influence in a variety of spheres of life. By contrast, the cosmopolitan's influence is monomorphic: it is restricted to the field in which he is consulted as an expert.

Currently there is speculation that, since two major types of influentials exist, there might possibly be more.

It is through the influentials that the mass media exert an important indirect influence. The influentials have a higher contact rate with the media and, hence, reflect this contact when passing on information to their circle of influencees.

Berelson and Steiner (1964: 550) suggest that (1) the more messages one directs to influentials, rather than influencees, the more effective the messages are likely to be, and (2) that word-of-mouth messages from an immediate and trusted source are typically more effective than are media messages from a remote and trusted source, despite the prestige of the latter.

53 | ADOPTION CURVE

THE INCREASING acceptance of an idea or product from its introduction until its complete adoption can be represented by a bell-shaped curve. This curve represents both time and number. It is, then, a graphic presentation of the flow of information and related social factors.

For instance, approximately 14 years elapsed between the introduction of hybrid seed corn and its adoption by most farmers. Approximately 20 months elapsed between the introduction of a new drug and its adoption by most doctors.

A synthesis of various adoption studies provides the following adopter categories:

Innovators. The first to adopt. Innovators are neither inventors or necessarily style setters; rather, the role of the innovator is to introduce the particular idea.

Influentials. The second group to adopt—and the most important—are the influentials, or opinion leaders. The role of the influential is crucial to the adoption process, for he legitimizes the idea to the population as a whole. That is, the fact that the influential has adopted the idea makes it acceptable for others to do so. If the influentials are not receptive to the idea introduced by the innovator, the adoption process will abort.

Early Majority. This group gets its social cues from the influentials, who have now made legitimate certain new behavior.

Late Majority. The second half of the broad category of majority, this group can take its social cues from either the influentials or the early majority.

Laggards. Members of this group have three sources for reference. Thus they may look to the group which adopted the innovation just ahead of them—the late majority—or turn directly to an influential or an early majority.

Die-hards. In theory the die-hards never capitulate to the new

8 | Informal Channels of Communication.   16 | Mass Communication.   52 | Influentials.

idea—but in reality, of course, they are behaving to some earlier idea. In some areas there are no die-hards. In medicine, for example, when old drugs are taken off the market there is no opportunity to be a die-hard, only a laggard.

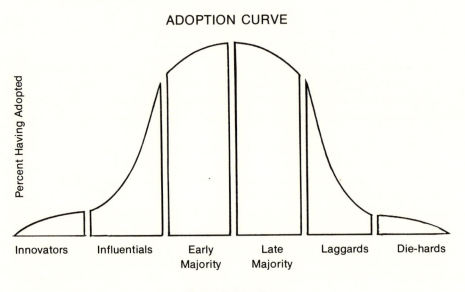

ADOPTION CURVE

Percent Having Adopted

Innovators Influentials Early Majority Late Majority Laggards Die-hards

Time of Adoption

54 | USES AND GRATIFICATIONS APPROACH

THE USES and gratifications approach to studies of mass communication developed as an alternative to the failure of a good deal of communication research to produce direct evidence of media effects on audience members. Particularly it became—by those researchers who had adopted the functions approach to the mass media—an avenue to explain the high levels of media consumption.

This approach contends that the interaction of people with the mass media can most often be explained by the *uses* to which they put the media content and/or the *gratifications* which they receive.

An early advocate was Katz, who argued the need for communication researchers to concentrate less on what the mass media was doing to the people ("effects") and to concentrate more on what the people were doing *with* the mass media. Even the most potent of the mass media, said Katz (1959), could not ordinarily influence an individual who has "no use" for it in the social and psychological environment in which he lives. Davison, too, was suggesting that many communication findings made more sense if viewed as a link between the individual and his society. The effects of mass communication, he said (Davison, 1959), can be explained in terms of the role they play in enabling people to bring about more satisfying relations between themselves and the world around them.

McQuail (1969:71) cites the uses and gratifications approach with two main advantages: (1) it helps both in understanding the significance and meaning of media use, and (2) it suggests a range of new intervening variables to be taken into account in the search for effects.

In summary, he notes:

It may be argued that until now the achievement of work along these lines [uses and gratifications approach] has been limited, and confined to demonstrating that people do bring needs to the mass media and are guided in their viewing, listening or reading by a set of expectations and looked-for gratifications; to showing that these needs partly originate in personality or in social circumstances; and to justifying an effort to take account of audience needs in any study of communication effects. . . . However, the amount of agreement reached amongst different investigators is really very striking, particularly on the nature and distribution of the gratifications involved. The gratifications revealed most often in a number of different studies of mass media include: the acquisition of news and information either about the wider, or the immediate environment; the provision of escape or release from anxiety, loneliness, tension, personal troubles, usually into a fantasy world, often by the mechanism of identification with hero or heroine; the offering of support, reassurance and an increase in self-esteem; help given in social interaction, as a topic of conversation, etc.; the provision of a ritualistic accompaniment to daily activities which "brackets" the day, sets the mood, maintains a familiar environment. (McQuail, 1969:74–75.)

55 | INFORMATION THEORY

OF THE THREE basic approaches to human communication (see "Communication"), information theory represents that body of scientific endeavor Smith labels mathematical. This branch of study first arose in telegraphy, with the need to specify precisely the *capacity* of some system of telecommunication to transmit information.

Consequently, the chief investigators in information theory are found in the engineering and physical sciences. Such investigators are not interested in the purposes of messages—whether they be gossip, major news stories, or a passing rumor. Rather, they are concerned with the correct transmission of signals (referred to as representations). "Mathematical communication theory," notes Cherry (1966:170), "concerns the signals alone, and their information content, abstracted from all specific human uses. It concerns not the question 'What sort of information?' but rather 'How much information?'"

In short, information theory is concerned with the making of representations—i.e., symbolism in its most general sense (MacKay, 1969:161).

Smith (1966) assigns information theorists with a basic interest in the technical developments in telecommunication engineering, whose key orientation is analysis of information in terms of probability and statistics.

> The communication engineer considers a communication system as a device which can exist in any one of a certain number of possible states. He thinks of a message as something chosen out of a set of possible messages. By thinking this way, he can calculate precisely how much information his channel could carry in one minute and how much is represented by the message it is actually carrying. In this way it becomes meaningful to talk about the informational efficiency of a telephone channel and to compare the efficiency to a rival coding system. (MacKay, 1969:15.)

1 | Communication.   18 | Telecommunication.   56 | Cybernetics.
59 | Communication Research.

In such technical systems, says Cherry (1966:41), the commodity which is bought and sold is information capacity. It is defined strictly on a mathematical basis; hence, it is without any of the vagueness which arises when human beings or other biological organisms are regarded as communication systems. As a scientific discipline, information theory rose to prominence with the work of Shannon.

56 | CYBERNETICS

THE STUDY of cybernetics focuses on communication and control in the brain and nervous systems of organisms and machines. "It is the study of messages, and in particular of effective message control . . ." (Wiener, 1950:9), basically in the physiological and engineering domain.

Feedback is the central concept in this field of study. The word cybernetics is taken from the Greek term *kybernetes*, meaning steersman. Cybernetics, then, suggests the central role of a feedback mechanism in communication control.

The Second World War gave birth to modern cybernetics. During this time it was recognized that many of the ideas, principles, and methods of the communication engineer had applicability to other areas of investigation:

> The lead was taken by Norbert Wiener who, with Rosenblueth, called attention to the great generality of the concept of *feedback*, which had been studied intensively by communication engineers for twenty years, and emphasized that this concept provided a useful relationship between biological and physical sciences. . . . The simplest feedback systems with which most people are familiar are the Watt Steam Governor, which regulates the speed of a steam engine, and the thermostat, which controls the temperature of a room. The needs of the War forced attention to feedback theory with the urgency of developing automatic predictors, automatic gun-laying mechanisms, and many other automatic-following, "self-controlling," or "goal-seeking" systems. Wiener and Rosenblueth called attention to the need for a general study that would cover not only these automatic mechanisms but also certain aspects of physiology, the central nervous system, and the operation of the brain, and even certain problems in economics concerning the theory of booms and slumps.
>
> The common thread linking these topics, whether mechanical, biological, or electrical, is the idea of communication of information and the setting up of self-stabilizing control action. (Cherry, 1966:57–58.)

In summary, as Wiener (1968) explains, cybernetics is a word coined to describe this new field of study. It brings together under one term what in a human context is sometimes described as thinking and in engineering is known as control and communication. In other words, says Wiener, cybernetics attempts to find the common elements in the functioning of automatic machines and of the human nervous system. It seeks to develop a theory which will cover the entire field of control and communication in machines and in living organisms. (There is a good deal of activity going on today under the title of cybernetics which is not cybernetics.)

Today cybernetics is often viewed as the science of data transformation in complex control systems and systems of information processing (Glushkor, 1969:47).

57 | POLLS

FOR NEARLY a half-century now, established polling agencies have been surveying the opinions of the American people. During this time, too, the polls have received both praise and blame.

> The word "poll" comes from the Middle English *polle*, meaning "top of the head," the part that showed when heads were being counted. Today, a *poll tax* is a head tax; the *polls* are where the heads are counted; and a poll is a counting of a sampling of heads, selected at random or by prearrangement, to reflect the opinion of a given populace. (Safire, 1968:345.)

A poll is a special descriptive survey of public opinion. A sample of some defined population, usually representing (but not limited to) the total adult population of the country, is queried. The sample members' opinions of varied political issues are then determined.

From the viewpoint of society, opinion polls serve such useful purposes as determining people's public concerns and keeping track of public opinion trends. From the viewpoint of candidates for political office, they permit a candidate to maximize his potential strength, determine the most appropriate context in which to address an issue, and target an opponent's weaknesses (Roll and Cantril, 1972:39–63).

Pollster is the name given to those who measure this public opinion, the term itself a relatively new one (since World War II). Among those in the field, however, the more preferred name is public opinion analyst.

In earlier years political polls were quite unsophisticated and sometimes highly inaccurate. In recent years opinion polls have become highly sophisticated and highly accurate, depending on probability sampling. In such sampling every individual in the population under study has an equal or known chance of being included in the sample. Through the principles of statistics, pollsters calculate the chances that the sample drawn actually is representative of the population being studied. The term "sampling error" is used to describe

16 | Mass Communication.   20 | Political Communication.
42 | Public Opinion.   43 | Public Opinion Process.   48 | Mass Society/Mass Culture.

scientifically how much the sample results can be expected to differ from the results that would be obtained if everyone in the population were interviewed.

Over the years, critics have noted shortcomings in public opinion polls. They have pointed out, for example, that polls ignore the fact that people are reluctant to reveal to untrusted strangers their deeply held, private sentiments. Also, they have observed that polls fail to take into account the knowledge behind people's preferences, or how strongly people may be committed to their choices. Thus Rogers, an early critic, questioned if polls measure what people think, observing that what men say to strangers, to acquaintances, to friends, to their wives, to themselves and in their sleep may vary a great deal. Moreover, he said pollsters are unable "to tell us the loudness of the yeses and the noes they say they hear" (Rogers, 1949:38, 45).

Pollsters now try to measure intensity of people's opinions. One way is to employ a numerical scale. Thus, after a person has stated an opinion, he is asked to select a position on a 10-point scale best reflecting the strength of his opinion. Another method is to have the respondent indicate the intensity of his opinion by choosing from a series of possible verbal responses to an opinion statement. For example, verbal responses such as: Do you strongly agree? Mildly agree? Mildly disagree? Strongly disagree? (Roll and Cantril, 1972:124).

Critics have noted other problems in public opinion polls. A certain amount of so-called polling is faked, wholly or in part, with the predetermined results printed by a gullible press; leaks of favorable results of a private poll are made to the press in order to get better press coverage for a candidate or improved financial support—or by releasing news favorable to an incumbent during the polling period in order to improve his rating in the poll.

Broadcast networks have been criticized for projecting winners of elections even while ballotting is continuing in some parts of the country.

Studies have indicated that early returns and computer predictions on election day do affect western voters. But the findings are unclear and partly contradictory (Hennessy, 1970:170).

Another criticism is that the political polls give unfair advantage to well-known personalities, that people may prefer such personalities to a pollster simply because they have heard of them.

Observers note also that often too much meaning is read into poll results. For example, a single poll tells nothing about how stable an opinion is, and a series of polls taken over a period of time may show rather significant shifts in opinion, and Blumer criticizes public opinion pollsters for simply aggregating the views of separate individuals and ignoring the fact that individuals and groups are not alike in their influence and thus their impact on public opinion (Blumer, 1954:73).

As Roll and Cantril put it, "a poll may be about as revealing as a snapshot in the backstretch of a horse race, telling nothing about what will happen at the finish line" (Roll and Cantril, 1972:121). Moreover, often there is a rush to obtain opinion data before opinions have really crystallized on an issue, a problem George Washington recognized two centuries ago:

> It is on great occasions only and after time has been given for cool and deliberate reflection that the real voice of the people can be known. (Roll and Cantril, 1972:118.)

Can polls replace voting and other government processes? Early pollsters were enthusiastic about what they thought polling could accomplish, and some apparently even thought it might become a new method of mass participation in government. One enthusiast declared that the polls may reflect the wishes of the electorate more faithfully than the elections themselves. This, he said, is because "variables enter in to keep some people away from the voting booths" (Rogers, 1949:4).

58 | CONTENT ANALYSIS

CONTENT ANALYSIS, according to Berelson's (1952) classic definition, is a research technique for the objective, systematic and quantitative description of the manifest content of communications.

Elaborating on this definition, Danielson (1963) notes that these key elements are:

Objective. The categories used to analyze content must be defined so precisely that anyone using them to analyze the same material would get the same results.

Systematic. The content to be analyzed must be selected in a predetermined, unbiased way. Thus, the researcher may not examine only those elements which fit his hypothesis.

Quantitative. Results are expressed numerically, such as in frequency distributions, contingency tables, correlation coefficients, ratios, percentages.

Manifest. Content is analyzed for what it says, not for the meaning "between the lines."

However, since Berelson defined content analysis in 1952, some content analysts have shifted their focus, becoming more concerned with the process and effects of communication rather than with the message itself. Accordingly, their major concern, they say, is to draw inferences. Carney observes:

> Nobody can argue from a communication to its effects without making inferences, . . . In fact, it is precisely this concern which distinguishes content analysis from an index, a concordance or concise abridgement or a precis. Content analysis always involves relating or comparing findings to some standard, norm or theory. It does so to discover latent attributes (in describing a communications flow, for instance) or to infer characteristics (in analyzing personality from writings which set out that person's perceptions).

Thus, Carney notes this definition "keeps coming to the fore,"

> Content analysis is any technique for making inferences by objectively and systematically identifying specified characteristics of messages. (Carney, 1972:5.)

5 | Message.   17 | Mass Media.   59 | Communication Research.

Communications content is studied for several reasons. From such study, inferences may be made about the message sender: about his intelligence, personality, attitudes, motives, values and goals, about the groups to which he belongs or desires to belong and their influence on him.

Also, the message has potential effects. Thus journalists, behavioral scientists, and laymen alike want to know what kind of messages are noticed, what kind are understood, what kind are remembered, what kind cause people to act.

In content analysis, random samples of material are commonly analyzed rather than the total space of a newspaper, book or magazine—or the total time on radio or television.

Though it dates back to the 1920's, content analyses continue to be popular. Present day content analysis makes use of computers, and stresses hypothesis testing instead of descriptive research. Another new trend is the use of content analysis in experimenting with such things as new advertising copy ideas (Danielson, 1963).

Content analysis has been used for purposes as varied as inferring enemy intentions from war-time propaganda to settling questions of disputed authorship. It has been applied not only to the mass media but to pottery fragments and psychoanalytic interviews. It has used instruments as simple as the wooden ruler, as complex as the multi-million dollar computer. It has dealt with measurement problems, ranging from counting column inches on the front page of a local newspaper to assessing the degree of "need achievement" in literary products of various cultures (Holsti, 1967:1).

Some have objected that content analysis is an over elaborate way of doing what a good historian or literary scholar does intuitively, that content analysis is no more certain than impressionistic reading, that it cannot deal with the total message, only the written document.

Carney rejects these criticisms. He sums up the matter this way:

"Impressionistic reading and inferring produces slipshod results. Content analysis gets infinitely better results, but at the cost of infinitely more painstaking labor. True, some forms of content analysis involve less work than others. It is easier to perform a word count or a count of spatial and typographical emphasis than it is to do a count of the occurrence of a complicated theme, for example. But the kind of inference possible is related to the kind of content analysis employed. Simple, straightforward counts most often allow only simple, straightforward inferences. The benefits have to be offset against labor costs involved. Sometimes there are prohibitive, given the actual time at the analysts' disposal." (Carney, 1972:16.)

59 | COMMUNICATION RESEARCH

COMMUNICATION RESEARCH is the scientific investigation of the communicative process. By scientific is meant that the investigation is a systematic, controlled, empirical, and critical examination of the supposed relationships of the variables involved. Historically, these investigations have been conducted in two broad areas, (1) mass communication or journalism research, and (2) face-to-face or interpersonal communication research. In either area, however, the research objective is the same: to contribute to the body of knowledge concerning all types of human communication, with the ultimate goal of prediction.

For the most part, mass communication research has concerned itself with studies in three general categories.

1. *Mass communication as a social institution*—its organization, its social control, its place in social structure and function, its audiences, its responsibilities and performance.

2. *The conditions of its effectiveness*—the choice of channels, the nature of messages, the self-selection of the audiences, the nature of attention, the problem of transmitting meaning, how group structure and predispositions influence the effect of a message on an audience.

3. *The nature and evidence of effects*—what mass communication does to the individual life, and what it contributes to social change or lack of change. (Schramm, 1958:5–6.)

Interpersonal communication research has tended to focus on the small group with emphasis on (1) the communicator, (2) the social context, (3) the channels employed, (4) verbal and nonverbal interaction, and (5) therapeutic communication. (Barnlund, 1968.)

Communication research is wide in scope; it crosses many disciplines. Schramm (1958:6) notes that the research task is not made easier by setting up artificial barriers between research efforts:

1 | Communication.   32 | Mass Communication Activities.   60 | Traditions in Communication Research.

The task ahead is rather to break down such barriers as already exist; to cross the imaginary borders (as the best researchers do now, and with ease and acceptance); to make use of the training of the psychologist, the sociologist, and others; to draw on the insights of the learning theorist, the psycholinguist, the psychiatrist, the specialist in small-group research, the student of propaganda and public opinion, the student of decision theory, and all the others who have some contribution to make to these problems; and to share with them our own particular insights, . . . for the widest possible exploration in other fields where our problems are under study, and for the maximum number of interchanges and alliances with other scholars working on these problems.

Brooks (1970:3) summarizes communication research this way:

The behavioral researcher studying communication works like any other scientist. He gathers facts about communication behavior, verifies his data, and subjects his interpretations to rigorous tests. The business of the behavioral scientist in communication is to predict and explain human communicative behavior. The broad, major questions he seeks to answer are these: Why do people communicate as they do? How can certain results of communicative events be explained? How can the behavioral scientist help individuals communicate more effectively? How can one modify communicative behavior by training? To gain insight into these questions, the communication scientist, like any other scientist, has to make observations. He observes casually bits of communicative behavior as they occur about him, and he observes purposively communicative behavior in the laboratory with refined instruments under highly controlled conditions.

A variety of methods is used in researching communication processes. These include:

1. The historical-critical method, in which documents are used to reconstruct what happened and criticize and compare.

2. The descriptive-analytic method, in which survey research and documentary evidence are used to determine what sorts of variables appear to bear relationships to one another.

3. Case studies in which intensive probes are made into one or a few important instances of communication or important sources of messages with the hope of generating realistic hypotheses for future study.

4. Field experimental studies, in which the controls of the laboratory and the realism of the natural setting are wedded as well as possible to determine the relationship of important variables or to assess the relative effectiveness of various messages, channels, systems or approaches to communication.

5. The ex post facto method, which involves observing an existing situation and searching back through data for plausible causes.

6. The controlled experiment, in which a communication treatment is compared for effectiveness with some control or set of controls to determine probable impacts.

As in the social sciences generally, descriptive and inferential statistics are employed in the analysis of data gathered under control conditions. Questionnaires, interviews, projective tests, standardized tests, attitude scales, semantic differential techniques, observational techniques and even physiological measures such as galvanic skin response are utilized.

60 | TRADITIONS IN COMMUNICATION RESEARCH

COMMUNICATION RESEARCH can be taken to encompass a variety of humanistic, critical, philosophic, historical, and scientific studies. Within this scope, there have been a number of traditions emerge in communication research in the United States. Some of the more important ones include:

1. Experiments on the factors involved in inducing change in human attitudes through manipulation of message factors. Carl I. Hovland was one of the seminal researchers in this area and from his work has grown a large body of research in what has been called scientific rhetoric—that is, rhetorical principles supported by scientific findings.

2. Closely related to this is a broad and diverse body of research and theorizing focusing on the social psychological aspects of communication and including theorists and researchers from George H. Mead through Kurt Lewin, Leon Festinger, Muzifer Sherif to R. D. Laing. Sherif and Hovland collaborated in some of the last research Hovland completed, thus the ties are close. But they also extend in three other directions: small group, sociological, and psychiatric.

3. Hugh Duncan (symbolism and social order), Irving Goffman (interaction analysis), and Herbert Blumer (symbolic interaction) represent three somewhat divergent sociological approaches to communication. All of them would acknowledge important but somewhat different intellectual debts to Mead. Other sociological traditions in communication are found among those who study complex organizations and those who study diffusion of information and innovations. Linkages to some concerns typical of anthropologists are also evident in sociological studies, for anthropologists are concerned with cultural and linguistic diffusion and many of them are convinced that communication is the cement that holds societies together and the means whereby culture transmission occurs across generations. In addition to sociology, a strong research link occurs between anthropology and linguistics, and, via psycholinguistics, to psychology.

59 | Communication Research.

4. Research and theorizing in the psychiatric and counseling professions have contributed to the understanding of two-person communication in long-term, intimate settings. Such research has extended to marital and family communication. Prominent researchers in this area include Bateson (also known for his anthropological contributions), Ruesch, Meerloo, Watzlawick, and such popular writers as Berne.

5. Small group research has tended toward the discovery of the dynamics of discussion and task accomplishment among both temporary and long-term groups. Researchers in this area include Fiedler, Leavitt, Bales, Bavelas, Kelley, and Thibaut.

6. Psycholinguistics research and the investigation of the processes of language development constitute another important body of communication research. Psychologists such as Osgood, G. A. Miller, and Rommetveit dominate in this area, focusing on such topics as connotative and denotative meaning, short-term memory, message context, and language acquisition.

7. Stimulated by the theorizing of Heider, Cartwright and Zander, and especially Theodore Newcomb, a recent and vigorous body of research has arisen dealing with the manner in which people "co-orient" to other people and symbolic objects simultaneously. Co-orientation research draws upon the work in empathy done by psychometricians, upon the efforts of the counseling professions, and upon mass media research in its concern for the manner in which messages from the media are processed in interpersonal settings by families and close friends. Steven Chaffee and Jack McLeod are prominent in this tradition.

8. Research on the impact of the mass media on various public information campaigns and on the process of voter persuasion enjoys a tradition begun by Lazarsfeld and his co-workers.

Other traditions include those important developments in sociolinguistics (Hymes, Fishman, Bernstein), philosophy (Lewis, Grice, Goldman, Vendler, Black et al.), cybernetics (Wiener, Ashby, Smith), systems theory (Ackoff), and other branches of psychology such as personality and child development. Finally, there has been a strong contribution in the areas of research methods and the theory of science, such as those by Guttman, Kuhn, and Polyani.

Though an incomplete listing, the scientists and research orientations noted here suggest the widespread interest in the communication process and the interpenetrating, cross-disciplinary character of research probes conducted in communication.

BIBLIOGRAPHY

Almond, Gabriel A. and G. Bingham Powell Jr., *Comparative Politics, A Developmental Approach.* Boston, Mass.: Little, Brown and Co., 1966.

———, and James S. Coleman (eds.), *The Politics of the Developing Areas.* Princeton, N.J.: Princeton University Press, 1960.

Bain, Read, "Category," in Gould and Kolb (eds.), *A Dictionary of the Social Sciences.* New York: The Free Press of Glencoe, 1964.

Barnlund, Dean C., *Interpersonal Communication: Survey and Studies.* Boston: Houghton Mifflin Company, 1968.

Bennett, John W., and Melvin M. Tumin, *Social Life.* New York: Alfred A. Knopf, Inc., 1949.

Berelson, Bernard, *Content Analysis and Communication Research.* Glencoe, Ill.: The Free Press of Glencoe, 1952.

———, and Gary A. Steiner, *Human Behavior.* New York: Harcourt, Brace and World, Inc., 1964.

Berkowitz, Leonard, *Social Psychology.* Glenview, Ill.: Scott, Foresman and Company, 1972.

Berlo, David K., *The Process of Communication.* New York: Holt, Rinehart and Winston, 1960.

Bernays, Edward L., *Public Relations.* Norman, Oklahoma: University of Oklahoma Press, 1952.

Best, James J., *Public Opinion: Micro and Macro.* Homewood, Ill.: Dorsey Press, 1973.

Blake, Reed H., "The Relationship Between Collective Excitement and Rumor Construction." *Rocky Mountain Social Science Journal.* Vol. 6, No. 2 (Oct. 1969), pp. 119–126.

Blumer, Herbert, "Public Opinion and Public Opinion Polling," in Daniel Katz, et al., *Public Opinion and Propaganda.* New York: Holt, Rinehart and Winston, 1954.

Bothe, B. J. W. and J. Van Koutrik, "The Teach-in as a Form of Political Communication," *Mens en Maatschappij.* Vol. 43, No. 3 (May–June 1968), pp. 258–272.

Brooks, Willian D., "Perspectives on Communication Research," in Emmert and Brooks (eds.), *Methods of Research in Communication.* New York: Houghton Mifflin Co., 1970.

Broom, Leonard, and Philip Selznick, *Principles of Sociology.* New York: Harper and Row, Publishers, Inc., 1970.

———, and Philip Selznick, *Sociology.* New York: Harper & Row, Publishers, Inc., 1963.

Burns, T., "A Meaning in Everyday Life." *New Society* (May 1967) No. 243.

Bush, Chilton R., *The Art of News Communication.* New York: Appleton-Century-Crofts, Inc., 1954.

Carney, Thomas F., *Content Analysis: A Technique for Systematic Inference From Communications.* Winnipeg: University of Manitoba Press, 1972.

Chafee, Zechariah, Jr., *Government and Mass Communications.* Vol. II. Chicago: University of Chicago Press, 1947.

Charnley, Mitchell V., *Reporting* 2nd ed. New York: Holt, Rinehart and Winston, Inc., 1966.

Cherry, Colin., *On Human Communication, A Review, A Survey, and A Criticism.* Cambridge, Mass.: The M.I.T. Press, 1966.

Copple, Neal, *Depth Reporting.* Englewood Cliffs, N.J.: Prentice-Hall, Inc., 1964.

Cutlip, Scott M. "Content and Flow of AP News," *Journalism Quarterly.* Vol. 31 (Fall 1954), pp. 434–446.

———, and Allen H. Center, *Effective Public Relations*, 2nd ed. Englewood Cliffs, N.J.: Prentice-Hall, Inc., 1958.

Danielson, Wayne, "Content Analysis in Communication Research," in Ralph O. Nafziger and David Manning White (eds.), *Introduction to Mass Communications Research.* Baton Rouge, La.: Louisiana State University Press, 1963.

Davison, W. Phillips and Alexander L. George, "An Outline for the Study of International Political Communication," in Heinz-Dietrich Fischer and John C. Merrill, *International Communication: Media, Channels, Functions.* New York: Hastings House, Publishers, 1970.

———, "On the Effects of Communication." *Public Opinion Quarterly.* Vol. 23 (Fall 1959), pp. 343–360.

DeFleur, Melvin L. *Sociology: Man in Society.* Glenview, Ill.: Scott, Foresman and Company, 1971.

———, *Theories of Mass Communication.* New York: David McKay Co., 1966.

Duncan, Hugh Dalziel, *Communication and Social Order.* London: Oxford University Press, 1962.

Duncan, Starkey, Jr. "Nonverbal Communication." *Psychological Bulletin.* Vol. 72, No. 2 (August 1969), pp. 118–137.

Emerson, Thomas I., *The System of Freedom of Expression.* New York: Random House, 1970.

Emery, Edwin, Phillip H. Ault, and Warren K. Agee, *Introduction to Mass*

Communications, 2nd ed. New York: Dodd, Mead, and Company, Inc., 1965.

Fagen, Richard R., *Politics and Communication*. Boston, Mass.: Little, Brown and Co., 1966.

Fischer, Heinz-Dietrich and John C. Merrill, *International Communication, Media, Channels, Functions*. New York: Hastings House, Publishers, Inc., 1970.

Gerald, J. Edward, *Social Responsibility of the Press*. Minneapolis, Minn.: University of Minnesota Press, 1963.

Gerbner, George, "Content Analysis and Critical Research in Mass Communication," in *AV Communication Review*, Vol. 6 (Spring, 1958), pp. 85–108.

Glushkor, V. M., "Contemporary Cybernetics," in Rose (ed.) *Survey of Cybernetics*. New York: Gordon and Breach, Science Publishers, 1969.

Goode, William J., *Vocabulary for Sociology*. Flushing, New York: Data-Guide, Inc., 1959.

Gordon, George N. and Irving A. Falk, *The War of Ideas*. New York, Hastings House, Publishers, Inc., 1973.

Gordon, George N., *Communications and Media: Constructing a Cross-Discipline*. New York: Hastings House, Publishers, Inc., 1975.

———, *The Languages of Communication*. New York: Hastings House, Publishers. 1969.

———, *Persuasion*. New York: Hastings House, Publishers, 1971.

Harriss, Julian, and Stanley Johnson, *The Complete Reporter*. New York: The Macmillan Company, 1965.

Hartley, Eugene L., and Ruth E. Hartley. "The Importance and Nature of Communication," *Fundamentals of Social Psychology*. New York: Alfred A. Knopf, Inc., 1961.

Head, Sydney W. "Intermedia Relationships, Symbiosis and Covergence," in Charles S. Steinberg (ed.), *Mass Media and Communication*, 2nd ed. New York: Hastings House, Publishers, 1972.

Hennessy, Bernard C., *Public Opinion*, 2nd ed. Belmont, California: Wadsworth Publishing Co., 1970.

Hersh, Seymour M., "The Story Everyone Ignores," in Michael C. Emery and Ted Curtis Smythe, *Readings in Mass Communication: Concepts and Issues in the Mass Media*. Dubuque, Iowa: Wm. C. Brown Co., Publisher, 1972.

Himes, Joseph S., *The Study of Sociology, An Introduction*. Glenview, Ill.: Scott, Foresman and Company, 1968.

Hoebel, E. Adamson, *Anthropology: The Study of Man*. New York: McGraw-Hill Book Co., 1966.

Hollander, Edwin P., *Principles and Methods of Social Psychology*. New York: Oxford University Press, 1967.

Holsti, Ole, *A National Conference on Content Analysis*. Philadelphia: Annenberg School of Communications, University of Pennsylvania, 1967.

Hook, Sidney, *The Paradoxes of Freedom*. Berkeley: University of California Press, 1962.

Hovland, C. I., "Social Communication," *Proceedings of the American Philosophical Society*, Vol. 92 (1948), pp. 371–375.

Hudon, Edward, *Freedom of Speech and Press in America*. Washington, D.C.: Public Affairs Press, 1963.

Hulteng, John L., *The Opinion Function: Editorial and Interpretive Writing for the News Media*. New York: Harper & Row, 1973.

Hyman, Herbert, *Survey Design and Analysis: Principles, Cases and Procedures*. New York: The Free Press, 1955.

Institute for Propaganda Analysis, "How to Detect Propaganda." *Propaganda Analysis*, Vol. I (November, 1937), pp. 1–4.

Izard, Ralph S., Hugh M. Culbertson and Donald A. Lambert, *Fundamentals of News Reporting*, 2nd ed. Dubuque, Iowa: Kendall/Hunt Publishing Co., 1973.

Johnson, Michael L., *The New Journalism*. Lawrence, Kansas: University Press of Kansas, 1971.

Katz, Elihu, "Mass Communication Research and the Study of Culture." *Studies in Public Communication*. Vol. 2 (Summer 1959), pp. 1–6.

Key, V. O. Jr., *Public Opinion and American Democracy*. New York: Alfred A. Knopf, 1961.

Klapper, Joseph T., *The Effects of Mass Communication*. New York: The Free Press, 1960.

Konvitz, Milton R., *First Amendment Freedoms*. Ithaca, New York: Cornell University Press, 1963.

Kreech, David, Richard S. Crutchfield and Egerton L. Ballachey. *Individual in Society*. New York: McGraw-Hill Book Company, Inc., 1962.

Lang, Kurt, and Gladys Engel Lang, *Collective Dynamics*. New York: Thomas Y. Crowell Company, 1967.

Lasswell, Harold D., "The Structure and Function of Communication in Society," in Byrson (ed.) *The Communication of Ideas*. New York: Harper and Row, 1948, pp. 37–51.

Lazarsfeld, Paul, and Robert Merton. "Mass Communication, Popular Taste and Organized Social Action," in Bryson (ed.), *The Communication of Ideas*. New York: Harper and Brothers, 1948.

Lerner, Daniel, "Communication Systems and Social Systems," in Schramm (ed.) *Mass Communications*. Urbana, Ill.: University of Illinois Press, 1960.

Lesly, Philip, *Public Relations Handbook*. Englewood Cliffs, N.J.: Prentice-Hall, Inc., 1950.

Lin, Nan, *The Study of Human Communication*. Indianapolis, Indiana: The Bobbs-Merrill Co., 1973.

Liston, Robert A., *The Right to Know, Censorship in America*. New York: Franklin Watts, Inc., 1973.

Lumsdaine, Arthur A., and Irving L. Janis, "Resistance to 'Counter-propaganda' Produced by one-sided and two-sided 'Propaganda' Presentations." *Public Opinion Quarterly*, Vol. 17 (Fall 1953), pp. 311–318.

MacDougall, Curtis D., *Interpretive Reporting*, 5th ed., London: The Macmillan Company, 1968.

MacKay, Donald M., *Information, Mechanism, and Meaning*. Cambridge, Mass.: The MIT Press, 1969.

Mandell, Maurice I. *Advertising*. Englewood Cliffs, N.J.: Prentice-Hall, Inc., 1968.

McDavid, John W. and Herbert Harari, *Social Psychology: Individuals, Groups, Societies*. New York: Harper & Row, Publishers, Inc., 1968.

McQuail, Denis, *Towards a Sociology of Mass Communication*. London: Collier-Macmillan Ltd., 1969.

Meiklejohn, Alexander, *Political Freedom, The Constitutional Powers of the People*. New York: Oxford University Press, 1965.

Mendelsohn, Harold, *Mass Entertainment*. New Haven, Conn.: College and University Press, 1966.

Merrill, Francis E., *Society and Culture*. Englewood Cliffs, N.J.: Prentice-Hall, Inc., 1969.

Merrill, John C., *The Imperative of Freedom: A Philosophy of Journalistic Autonomy*. New York: Hastings House, Publishers, Inc., 1974.

———, and Ralph L. Lowenstein, *Media, Messages and Men: New Perspectives in Communication*. New York: David McKay Co., Inc., 1971.

Merton, Robert K., *On Theoretical Sociology*. New York: The Free Press, 1957.

Mill, John Stuart, *On Liberty*. London: Longmans, Green, Reader & Dyer, 1869.

Miller, G. A., *Language and Communication*. New York: McGraw-Hill Book Company, Inc., 1951.

———, "The Psycholinguists." *Encounter*. Vol. 23, No. 1 (July 1964), pp. 29–37.

Miller, Gerald R. "On Defining Communication: Another Stab," in *Journal of Communication*, Vol. 16, No. 2 (June 1966), pp. 88–99.

Rao, L. Jaganmohan, "Communication Channels in the Innovation-Decision Process: Some Dimensions of Channel Concept and Tentative Hypotheses," paper delivered at the International Communication Association meetings, Atlanta, Ga., 1972.

Redding, W. Charles and George A. Sanborn, *Business and Industrial Communication: A Sourcebook*. New York: Harper & Row, Publishers, Inc., 1964.

Rogers, Lindsay, *The Pollsters: Public Opinion, Politics and Democratic Leadership*. New York: Alfred A. Knopf, 1949.

Roll, Charles W. Jr. and Albert H. Cantril, *Polls, Their Use and Misuse in Politics*. New York: Basic Books, 1972.

Roper, Burns W., *Emerging Profiles of Television and Other Mass Media: Public Attitudes, 1959–1967*. New York: Television Information Office, 1967.

Safire, William, *Politics: An Anecdotal Dictionary of Catchwords, Slogans and Political Usage*. New York: Random House, 1968.

Schramm, Wilbur, *Men, Messages and Media: A Look at Human Communication*. New York: Harper and Row, Publishers, Inc., 1973.

————, *Mass Communications*. Urbana, Ill.: University of Illinois Press, 1960.

————, "The Challenge to Communication Research," in Nafziger, Ralph O. and David M. White (eds.), *Introduction to Mass Communications Research*. Baton Rouge, La.: Louisiana State University Press, 1958.

Shibutani, Tamotsu, *Improvised News: A Sociological Study of Rumor*. Indianapolis, Indiana: The Bobbs-Merrill Company, Inc., 1966.

Siebert, Fred S., Theodore Peterson and Wilbur Schramm, *Four Theories of the Press*. Urbana, Ill.: University of Illinois Press, 1963.

Smith, Alfred B., *Communication and Culture*. New York: Holt, Rinehart and Winston., 1966.

Thomas, Norman, *The Test of Freedom*. New York: W. W. Norton & Co., 1954.

Wagner, Richard V. and John J. Sherwood, *The Study of Attitude Change*. Belmont, California: Brooks/Cole Publishing Company, 1969.

Waldrop, A. Gayle, *Editor and Editorial Writer*, 3rd ed. Dubuque, Iowa: William C. Brown Company Publishers, 1967.

Westley, Bruce H., *News Editing*, 2nd ed. Boston: Houghton Mifflin Co., 1972.

White, David Manning, "The 'Gatekeeper,' A Case Study in the Selection of News." *Journalism Quarterly*, Fall, 1950, 383–90.

Wiener, Norbert, "Cybernetics in History," in Buckley (ed.), *Modern Systems Research for the Behavior Scientist*. Chicago: Aldine Publishing Company, 1968.

————, *The Human Use of Human Beings: Cybernetics and Society*. Boston: Houghton Mifflin Co., 1950.

Wilson, Everett K., *Sociology: Rules, Roles, and Relationships*. Homewood, Illinois: The Dorsey Press, 1966.

Wirth, Louis, "Consensus and Mass Communication," *American Sociological Review*, Vol. 13, No. 1 (February, 1948), pp. 5–26.

Wright, Charles R., "Functional Analysis and Mass Communication," *Public Opinion Quarterly*, Vol. 24 (Winter, 1960), pp. 606–620.

————, *Mass Communication*. New York: Random House, 1959.

AUTHOR INDEX

SUBJECT INDEX

(Page numbers in boldface type indicate main treatment or definition.)

155